TRAUMATIC GRIEF:
DIAGNOSIS, TREATMENT, AND PREVENTION

TRAUMATIC GRIEF: DIAGNOSIS, TREATMENT, AND PREVENTION

Selby C. Jacobs, M.D., M.P.H.

USA	Publishing Office:	BRUNNER/MAZEL *A member of the Taylor & Francis Group* 325 Chestnut Street Philadelphia, PA 19106 Tel: (215) 625-8900 Fax: (215) 625-2940
	Distribution Center:	BRUNNER/MAZEL *A member of the Taylor & Francis Group* 47 Runway Road, Suite G Levittown, PA 19057 Tel: (215) 269-0400 Fax: (215) 269-0363
UK		BRUNNER/MAZEL *A member of the Taylor & Francis Group* 1 Gunpowder Square London EC4A 3DE Tel: +44 171 583 0490 Fax: +44 171 583 0581

TRAUMATIC GRIEF: Diagnosis, Treatment, and Prevention

1 2 3 4 5 6 7 8 9 0

Printed by Hamilton Printing Co., Castleton, NY, 1999.

A CIP catalog record for this book is available from the British Library.

∞ The paper in this publication meets the requirements of the ANSI Standard Z39.48-1984 (Permanence of Paper).

Library of Congress Cataloging-in-Publication Data

Jacobs, Selby, 1939-
      Traumatic grief: diagnosis, treatment, and prevention/Selby C.
    Jacobs.
        p. cm. -- (The series in trauma and loss, ISSN 1090-9575)
     Includes bibliographical references and index.
     ISBN 0-87630-985-6 (alk. Paper). -- ISBN 0-87630-986-4 (alk.
    paper)
     1. Grief. 2. Bereavement--Psychological aspects. 3. Death-
   -Psychological aspects. I. Title. II. Series.
     [DNLM: 1. Grief. 2. Stress Disorders, Post-Traumatic. WM 170
    J16t 1999]
    RC455.4.L67J33 1999
    616.85'21--dc21
    DNLM/DLC
    For Library of Congress   98-32239
                                     CIP

ISBN 0-87630-986-4 (paper)
ISBN 0-87630-985-6 (case)
ISSN 1090-9575

DEDICATION

To Ann Blinn, Alicia Ann, and Kyra Rae

CONTENTS

Preface   XI
Acknowledgments   XIX

1   Attachment Behavior and Theory   1

Introduction to Attachment Theory   1
Attachment Behavior   2
Neurobiology of Affiliation   4
Separation Anxiety After a Loss   5
An Example of Separation Anxiety   7
Separation Anxiety and Normal Grief   8
Attachment Behavior and Psychopathology   10
Conclusion   11
References   12

2   Definition of Traumatic Grief as a Disorder   14

The Concept of Pathologic Grief   14
Consensus Diagnostic Criteria for Traumatic Grief   17
Comparison of Criteria for Traumatic Grief With Another Set
    of Published Criteria   20
Mental Disorders in DSM-IV and the Issue of Cultural
    Sanction   21
The Nature of Traumatic Grief   22
Conclusion and Definition of Traumatic Grief   24
References   25

3 **Diagnosis of Traumatic Grief**   27

Death of a Significant Other and Symptoms of Separation
    Anxiety: Criterion A   27
Bereavement Specific Symptoms of Traumatization by a
    Death: Criterion B   29
Severity of Symptoms for Both Criteria A and B   31
Issue of Duration: Criterion C   32
Impairment in Psychosocial Functioning: Criterion D   33
Variations in the Pattern of Traumatic Grief   33
Anniversaries of the Death   34
Associated Descriptive Features   34
Associated Physical Findings and General Medical
    Conditions   35
Associated Laboratory Findings   36
Course and Prognosis   36
Differential Diagnosis of Traumatic Grief   36
Conclusion   42
References   42

4 **Comorbidity: Psychiatric Disorders Associated with
Traumatic Grief**   45

Associated Psychiatric Disorders   45
Traumatic Grief: Is it Old Wine in a New Bottle?   52
Diagnosis of a Comorbid Disorder During Bereavement:
    Special Considerations   53
Clinical Examples   54
Conclusion   56
References   57

5 **Treatment of Traumatic Grief**   60

A Philosophy of Treatment   60
Overview of Treatment   61
Psychopharmacology   62
Psychotherapy   67
Conclusion   73
References   73

6	**A Diagnosis/Treatment Algorithm for Traumatic Grief**	**76**

A Diagnosis/Treatment Algorithm for Traumatic Grief   76
Personal Notes on Psychotherapy and Psychotropic Drugs   81
Clinical Narrative   83
More Notes on Treatment From the Case Examples   84
Conclusion   87
References   87

7	**Epidemiology and Prevention of Traumatic Grief**	**89**

Prevalence and Incidence of Traumatic Grief   89
Age and Gender Variation in Grief and Traumatic Grief   91
Social and Cultural Issues   91
Utilization of Services and Costs   93
Risks Factors for Traumatic Grief   94
Prevention of Traumatic Grief   96
Conclusion   97
References   98

8	**Conclusion and Future Directions**	**102**

The Costs and Benefits of Attachment   102
The Clinical Challenge   103
Review of the Text   103
Natural Processes, Healing, and the Helping Professional   104
Future Developments   105
A Dimensional Approach to Diagnosis   106
Other Types of Losses   106
References   107

PREFACE

The death of a family member or intimate friend exposes the bereaved person to a high risk for several types of psychiatric disorders. These include Major Depressions, Panic Disorders, Generalized Anxiety Disorders, Post-traumatic Stress Disorders, and increased alcohol use and abuse (Bornstein, Clayton, Halikas, Maurice, Robins, 1973; Jacobs, Hansen, Berkman, Kasl, Ostfeld, 1989; Jacobs, Hansen, Kasl, Ostfeld, Berkman, Kim, 1990; Schut, de Keijser, van den Bout, Dijhuis, 1991; Zisook, Shuchter, Mulvilhill, 1990; Zisook and Shuchter, 1991, 1993; Breslau et al., 1998). In addition to these potential complications of bereavement, there is renewed and current interest in pathologic grief as a nosologic entity deserving recognition. Such a new diagnosis defined in terms of distortions of grief in reaction to a death would be distinct from Major Depression, Panic Disorder, and Post-traumatic Stress Disorder (Horowitz et al., 1997; Jacobs, 1993; Prigerson et al., 1995, 1997a and b).

Recently, two groups have proposed diagnostic criteria for pathologic grief. One presented criteria for Complicated Grief Disorder (Horowitz et al., 1997), and the other for Traumatic Grief (Prigerson, Maciejewski, Pilkonis, Wortman, Williams, Widiger, Davidson, Frank, Kupfer, Zisook, in press; Prigerson and Jacobs, in press). These two criteria sets, while differing in some respects, have considerable consistency, which suggests independent validation of each other. Soon, additional research and consensus groups hope to reconcile the differences, leading to a universal, single set of working diagnostic criteria.

Based on a series of studies on pathologic grief from which twin themes of separation anxiety and traumatic distress emerge, I refer to this new diagnostic entity as "Traumatic Grief". Chapter 2 explains the rationale for this choice in more detail.

This book reviews consensus diagnostic criteria for Traumatic Grief that were recently developed and published by a panel of experts organized by Dr. Holly Prigerson and colleagues, moderated by Dr. Charles Reynolds, III, and convened as a Traumatic Grief Work Group at the University of Pittsburgh Department of Psychiatry (Prigerson et al., in press; Prigerson and Jacobs, in press). Essentially, the book adopts the outline of Diagnostic and Statistical Manual IV (DSM-IV) for introducing the diagnosis of Traumatic Grief as a psychiatric disorder in adults. After defining the disorder, I discuss in detail the clinical use of the diagnostic criteria. Furthermore, to the extent that we understand these matters at this point, the text describes the associated descriptive features of Traumatic Grief, its differential diagnosis, and its clinical course. Next, I give attention to psychiatric disorders that can be associated with Traumatic Grief, in other words, the psychiatric comorbidity of Traumatic Grief, and the implications of comorbidity, as we understand it, preliminarily, for treatment. After discussing issues, I explore specific treatments for Traumatic Grief. While the literature on treatment is in an early stage of development, there are still important leads from systematic studies. This literature review leads to the development of a diagnosis/treatment algorithm based not only on the literature but also my own clinical experience. Before concluding, there is a review of the epidemiology and prevention of Traumatic Grief, including social and cultural variation in mourning, that places the disorder in a social and cultural context where it is optimally understood and treated. Through these steps, the book offers a first time comprehensive, albeit introductory, approach to thinking about Traumatic Grief.

I want to emphasize to the reader up front that the concept of Traumatic Grief is developing rapidly. The diagnostic criteria are not complete and final. Different diagnostic algorithms need to be tested extensively in the field over the next five years. The ideas about treatment are based on some assumptions, supported by some systematically collected data, and are therefore preliminary while awaiting more studies. Thus, this book cannot be used as a simple recipe-style manual for the next few years. Rather, it is intended as a timely introduction to rapidly breaking developments and a guide to following those developments, supplemented by the clinician's own experience and a critical reading of the literature as it emerges. I believe the diagnosis and treatment of Traumatic Grief deserves this attention.

☐ Perspective

Embarking on the journey of defining criteria and discussing treatment for the diagnosis of Traumatic Grief raises a fundamental question about whether it is wise to undertake this task at all (Averill and Nunley, 1993). Strong philosophical attitudes prevail in the medical community and in larger society that we should not interfere with the natural process of grief by introducing medicine, not to mention psychiatry, into it. On the other hand, there is a growing clinical science regarding the diagnosis and treatment of Traumatic Grief. In my opinion, the mounting evidence, which I will begin to review in chapter 2 and elaborate on in subsequent chapters, strongly indicates that the time has arrived to undertake the challenge of defining the disorder named Traumatic Grief and then outlining approaches to its treatment.

I believe that a scientific attitude using modern data and conservative judgment charts a course through the straits created by prevailing cultural beliefs and altruistic urges to help others in need at this time in their lives. Employing a scientific approach, this book will verify the concept of Traumatic Grief as a disorder characterized by a specific syndrome. It will describe how the syndrome is stable over time and is associated with functional impairment, coexisting medical and psychiatric morbidity, and a potential for disability. Also, the text will review the studies of several authors who have focused on "pathologic grief" during the 20th century. Usually, authors have chosen the rubric of pathologic grief as their title for this disorder and, less often, other names such as neurotic grief, atypical grief, or complicated grief. Whatever the name chosen, these studies contribute to our understanding of Traumatic Grief.

This book will begin by focusing on the personal and biologic processes of grief. Still, the diagnosis of Traumatic Grief must also be placed in a social and cultural context. In society, a dialectic exists between the person and the social environment through the structures and processes of status, roles, and attributions of meaning. Inevitably, there are potential social consequences of the choice to develop diagnostic criteria for Traumatic Grief. One of them is to move grief more into the domain of the personal and biologic. These consequences include a potential loss of shared meaning and coherence that the social and cultural environment provides as well as a threat to the role of natural family and self-help supports in resolving the difficulties posed by a death (Averill and Nunley, 1993). Therefore, as a counterpoint to the development of diagnostic criteria, the text will remind helping professionals of their responsibility to found their practice on a knowledge of normal grief, a broad theoretical model of psychopathology that encompasses not only personal but also social factors, and an awareness of the social context of bereavement with its varying ethnic prescriptions for how to cope with a loss.

Having said this, it might be helpful to the reader to add that the basic premise of the text, that universal diagnostic criteria can be developed, evokes an exercise in lumping, not splitting. Presumably, the criteria cut across social and cultural differences and are useful in a variety of countries and cultures. There is some evidence for this proposition that is discussed in chapter 7, though this assumption now ought to be tested systematically with the available consensus criteria.

☐ Theories and Models

Theories and models provide an important framework for understanding and investigating the nature of loss, grief, and the clinical complications of bereavement. Theory helps us to organize our observations with over-arching concepts. It offers a way to understand individual variation, including the distinction between normal and abnormal, and it provides a strategic platform for selecting problems to be solved in treatment or research.

Several theories have influenced the development of our understanding of bereavement during the 20th century. Psychoanalytic theory was the first to emerge. Psychoanalysis dominated American psychiatric thought about bereavement starting with the publication of *Mourning and Melancholia* in 1917 (Freud, 1953). Psychoanalytic theory, including Lindeman's seminal observations of the phenomena of grief (Lindeman, 1944), maintained a hegemony that lasted until the mid-1950s. Perhaps stemming from psychoanalysis's focus on the relationship between grief and depression, one current school of thought conceptualizes the clinical complications of bereavement within the framework of depression theory and practice (Clayton, 1990). Beginning in the 1950s, clinicians and scientists working in Great Britain began to formulate concepts about bereavement based on ethology and evolution and linked them to observations in children, adults, and other animal species, thereby working toward a new theory of attachment (Bowlby, 1969, 1973, 1980; Parkes, 1959). Another theoretical approach, which emerged in the 1970s and remains important, is stress theory. Stress theory focuses on the occurrence of a stressful event and the individual's efforts to cope with it (Horowitz, 1976). Also, during the 1970s, behavior therapists formulated behavioral models for understanding "pathologic grief" (Kavanaugh, 1990). Counterbalancing these theories that focus primarily on the individual, several social scientists have formulated social perspectives on grief. These emphasize the status, social roles, and social supports of bereaved persons as well as the attribution of meaning to a loss within a social context (Walker, MacBride, Vachon, 1977; Silverman, 1986; Rosenblatt, 1993; Averill and Nunley, 1993).

Each of these theoretical perspectives have strengths and weaknesses, advantages and disadvantages, and none encompasses the whole picture. Fortunately, they do not seem to me to be exclusive in many respects and, certainly, an intellectual dialectic between the personal and the social is necessary to mirror the integrated, psychosocial experience of the bereaved person living in society.

I have chosen to develop attachment theory as the main framework for thinking about death, grief, and bereavement in this book. I have found attachment theory most useful for my own work because of its objective, behavioral, personal, developmental, and cognitive strengths. I place attachment theory in the framework of a broad, medical model. A medical model emphasizes the clinical complications of bereavement as disease states (or disorders). A broad medical model encompasses an understanding of the environment through the disciplines of epidemiology and public health. Epidemiology focuses on the vectors of disease and on risk factors which can be socioenvironmental as well as personal. Moreover, preventive interventions are integral to a public health perspective. In addition, a broad medical model concerns itself with the efforts of the individual to cope and adapt to perceived threats while adapting to an environment changed by a loss. These advantages of a broad medical model compensate for some of the weaknesses and disadvantages of attachment theory. Together, in my opinion, attachment theory and a broad medical model provide a powerful, conceptual structure for understanding the problems posed by the diagnosis and treatment of Traumatic Grief.

☐ Outline of the Chapters

Chapter 1 provides an overview of attachment behavior as an integral part of the human repertory of behavior. In addition to a brief summary of salient elements of attachment theory, this chapter also covers recent neurobiologic studies of affiliation, discusses the concept of separation anxiety, and briefly summarizes a contemporary understanding of normal grief. Attachment theory provides a conceptual structure for thinking about psychopathology during bereavement. By acknowledging attachment theory in this chapter, I do not want to suggest that the subsequent material on diagnosis and treatment is only theoretically driven. On the contrary, as readers will realize as they progress through the text, the criteria presented and the review of treatment are empirically and clinically based.

Chapter 2 begins with a review of the development of ideas about pathologic grief in the 20th century. This is the conceptual history that leads to the formulation of diagnostic criteria for Traumatic Grief. Next, it reviews recent evidence supporting the feasibility and need for developing this new nosologic entity. This chapter discusses the choice of Traumatic Grief as a name for the disorder and introduces consensus criteria for the diagnosis of Traumatic Grief. This introduction includes a brief discussion of the nature of the disorder as we currently understand it. Finally, in response to a definitional issue raised in the *Diagnostic and Statistical Manual,* there is a discussion and rejection of the idea that the manifestations of Traumatic Grief are merely an expectable and culturally sanctioned response to death.

Chapter 3 discusses in detail the application of the new set of diagnostic criteria for Traumatic Grief developed at a recent consensus conference by a panel of experts. In this chapter, I evaluate the similarities and differences of the consensus criteria to another published set of criteria. Following the format established for disorders in DSM-IV, the chapter discusses physical findings and laboratory tests related to the disorder. Next, this chapter presents evidence for the chronic, unremitting course, if untreated, of the severe symptoms that characterize Traumatic Grief. Finally, this chapter reviews the differential diagnosis of Traumatic Grief.

Chapter 4 covers the comorbidity of Traumatic Grief, i.e., the other psychiatric disorders that occur during bereavement and are potentially associated with Traumatic Grief. These include Major Depression, anxiety disorders, and Post-traumatic Stress Disorders. The chapter provides a discussion of the possible relationships among the different types of psychopathology and the implications of comorbidity for treatment are introduced.

Chapter 5 reviews systematically evaluated, potentially specific treatments for Traumatic Grief. Since Traumatic Grief is a newly developing entity, I use some assumptions about the nature of the disorder and rely on studies designed to treat related disorders to find relevant evidence. This chapter examines both psychotherapeutic and pharmacological interventions. The text also covers briefly the role of mutual support groups in treatment and recovery.

Chapter 6 presents a diagnosis/treatment algorithm for Traumatic Grief, building on the discussion of chapters 3, 4, and 5 and integrating my experience from several years of practice. It is intended as a synthesis that integrates some of the technical aspects of the previous discussion and illustrates how to build individualized treatment plans at the proper level of intensity based on careful evaluation of each bereaved person. This chapter recommends an integrated framework using evidence-based treatments and depending on the needs and coping styles of particular patients as well as the phase of bereavement.

Chapter 7 reviews the incidence and prevalence of Traumatic Grief showing that huge numbers of bereaved persons are at risk each year. Review of this data establishes a particular and unique epidemiologic profile for Traumatic Grief. The unique epidemiologic profile serves as an additional validation of Traumatic Grief as a new and distinct nosologic entity. Emerging data on the utilization of services by persons with Traumatic Grief, as well as the potential cost offset of specific and focused treatment, emphasize the need for attention to this emerging disorder. Included in this chapter is an overview of the social and cultural variation of grief and its implications for treatment. Finally, this chapter offers an approach to prevention. The potential for an epidemiology of Traumatic Grief offers realistic opportunities for prevention. Opportunities exist both before and after a death. If primary prevention fails, there is still an opportunity for secondary prevention, that is, early intervention after the onset of a disorder to reduce the severity of illness and minimize the risk of consequent disability.

Chapter 8, the final chapter, briefly places Traumatic Grief in the context of a broader group of affiliative behaviors. This chapter emphasizes the need to understand and foster normal grief as a natural process, so as to enhance and not compromise natural healing processes. Furthermore, this chapter emphasizes that treatment ought to be implemented through the development of a clinical narrative of the illness and in a manner that cares for the person who is ill.

☐ References

Averill, J. R., Nunley, E. P. (1993). Grief as an emotion and as a disease: A social constructionist perspective. In M. S. Stroebe, W. Stroebe, R. O. Hansson (Eds.), *Handbook of bereavement: Theory, research, and intervention* (pp. 77–90). Cambridge, England: Cambridge University Press.

Bornstein, P. C., Clayton, P. J., Halikas, J. A., Maurice, W. L., & Robins, E. (1973). The depression of widowhood after thirteen months. *British Journal of Psychiatry, 122,* 561–566.

Bowlby, J. (1969). *Attachment and loss, vol 1: Attachment.* New York: Basic Books.

Bowlby, J. (1973). *Attachment and loss, vol 2: Separation.* New York: Basic Books.

Bowlby, J. (1980). *Attachment and loss, volume 3: Loss, sadness and depression.* New York: Basic Books.

Breslau, N., Kessler, R. C., Chilcoat, H. D., Schultz, L. R., Davis, G. C., & Andreski, P. (1998). Trauma and posttraumatic stress disorder in the community. *Arch Gen Psychiat, 55,* 626–632.

Clayton, P. J. (1990). Bereavement and depression. *Journal of Clinical Psychiatry, 51,* 34–38.

Freud, S. (1953). Mourning and melancholia. In J. Strachey (Ed. and Trans.), *The standard edition, volume 14* (pp. 243–258). London: Hogarth.

Horowitz, M. J. (1976). *Stress response syndromes.* New York: Jason Aronson, Inc.

Horowitz, M. J., Siegel, B., Holen, A., Bonnano, G. A., Milbrath, C., & Stinson, C. H. (1997). Diagnostic criteria for complicated grief disorder. *American Journal of Psychiatry, 154,* 904–910.

Jacobs, S. C., Hansen, F. F., Berkman, L., Kasl, S., Ostfeld, A. (1989). Depressions of bereavement. *Comprehensive Psychiatry, 30,* 218–224.

Jacobs, S. C., Hansen, F. F., Kasl, S. V., Ostfeld, A., Berkman, L., Kim, K. (1990). Anxiety disorders during acute bereavement: Risk and risk factors. *Journal of Clinical Psychiatry, 51,* 269–274.

Jacobs, S. (1993). *Pathologic grief: Maladaptation to loss.* Washington, DC: American Psychiatric Press.

Kavanagh, D. J. (1990). Towards a cognitive-behavioural intervention for adult grief reactions. *British Journal of Psychiatry, 157,* 373–383.

Lindeman, E. (1944). Symptomatology and management of acute grief. *American Journal of Psychiatry, 101,* 141–148.

Parkes, C. M. (1959). Morbid grief reactions: A review of the literature. Dissertation for Doctorate of Psychological Medicine. University of London.

Prigerson, H. G., Frank, E., Kasl, S. V., Reynolds, C. F., Anderson, B., Zubenko, G. S., Houck, P. R., George, C. J., & Kupfer, D. J. (1995). Complicated grief and bereavement-related depression as distinct disorders: Preliminary empirical validation in elderly bereaved spouses. *American Journal of Psychiatry, 152,* 22–30.

Prigerson, H. G., Bierhals, A. J., Kasl, S. V., Reynolds, C. F., Shear, M. K., Day, N., Beery, L. C., Newsom, J. T., & Jacobs, S. (1997a). Traumatic Grief as a risk factor for mental and physical morbidity. *American Journal of Psychiatry, 154,* 617–623.

Prigerson, H. G., Shear, M. K., Frank, E., Beery, L. C., Silberman, R., Prigerson, J., Reynolds, C. F. (1997b). Clinical case conference: Traumatic Grief: A case of loss-induced trauma. *American Journal of Psychiatry, 154,* 1–5.

Prigerson, H. G., Shear, M. K., Jacobs, S. C., Reynolds, C. F., Maciejewski, P. K., Pilkonis, P., Wortman, C., Williams, J. B. W., Widiger, T. A., Davidson, J., Frank, E., Kupfer, D. J., Zisook, S.: Consensus Criteria for Traumatic Grief: A preliminary empirical test. *British Journal of Psychiatry,* in press.

Prigerson, H. G., Jacobs, S. C. (in press). Diagnostic criteria for Traumatic Grief: Conceptual issues, critical appraisal, and an empirical test. In M. S. Stroebe, W. Stroebe, R. O. Hansson & H. Schut (Eds.), *New handbook of bereavement: Consequences, coping and care.* Washington, DC: American Psychological Association Press.

Rosenblatt, P. C. (1993). The social context of private feelings. In M. S. Stroebe, W. Stroebe, & R. O. Hansson (Eds.), *Handbook of bereavement: Theory, research, and intervention* (pp. 102–111). New York: Cambridge University Press.

Schut, H. A. W., de Keijser, J. van den Bout, J. & Dijhuis, J. H. (1991). Post-traumatic symptoms in the first year of conjugal bereavement. *Anxiety Research, 4,* 225–234.

Silverman, P. (1986). *Widow to widow.* New York: Springer Publishing.

Walker, K. N., MacBride, A., & Vachon, M. L. S. (1977). Social support networks and the crisis of bereavement. *Social Science and Medicine, 2,* 35–41.

Zisook, S., Shuchter, S. R., & Mulvilhill, M. (1990). Alcohol, cigarette, and medication use during the first year of widowhood. *Psychiatric Annals, 20,* 318–326.

Zisook, S., Shuchter, S. R. (1991). Depression through the first year after the death of a spouse. *American Journal of Psychiatry, 148,* 1346–1352.

Zisook, S., Shuchter, S. R. (1993). Uncomplicated bereavement. *Journal of Clinical Psychiatry, 54,* 365–372.

ACKNOWLEDGMENTS

While several persons made contributions to writing this text, if Robert Cole, the Chief Operating Officer of the Connecticut Mental Health Center, had not covered my responsibilities while I was on academic leave for six months, I would not have had the opportunity to complete this endeavor. I want to acknowledge his good friendship, enormous talent and essential contribution to making this text possible.

I also want to acknowledge Holly Prigerson, whose recent studies served as a major stimulus for my endeavor. Indeed, her scholarship provides a foundation for the new, consensus criteria for the diagnosis of Traumatic Grief. She is asking and scientifically pursuing ground-breaking questions in the fields of thanatology, traumatology, and psychosocial stress epidemiology. A dialogue with her, including her willingness to read several drafts of chapters, not to mention her numerous, insightful publications, helped me to develop and focus the presentation in the text.

Ms. Sheila Meyers was instrumental in preparing and proofreading the text and bibliography as well as helping to organize work on the manuscript after I returned from academic leave. I would like to acknowledge her contribution. She is undoubtedly one of the most able, constructive, careful, and helpful persons with whom I have had the pleasure of collaborating.

Other colleagues too numerous to mention have contributed over several years to the development of the data and ideas in the text. Without naming each of them individually, I would like to acknowledge them and our collective effort as a final note.

CHAPTER

1

Attachment Behavior and Theory

Given the central and pervasive importance of attachment behavior and attachment theory in modern thinking about personal relationships and loss, the text begins with a brief overview of them. The introduction to attachment behavior and theory in this chapter serves as a conceptual framework for the rest of the text. For example, the task of defining Traumatic Grief in chapter 2 builds on this foundation. Similarly, some of the specific criteria used for the diagnosis of Traumatic Grief and discussed in chapter 3 derive from the discussion of separation anxiety introduced her. The discussion of treatments in chapters 5 and 6 also relies in part on concepts introduced here and incorporated into the definition and diagnosis of Traumatic Grief. In addition to the foundation that attachment behavior and theory provide for understanding the diagnosis and treatment of Traumatic Grief, growing knowledge of attachment behavior has been partly responsible for the burgeoning number of neurobiologic studies of affiliation, which are reviewed briefly below.

☐ Introduction to Attachment Theory

Attachment theory stems from evolution theory and ethology, which is the scientific study of animal behavior (Darwin, 1872). Ethologic studies document attachment behavior in a variety of animal species, including primates and humans (Carter, Lederhendler, & Kirkpatrick, 1997). The main architect of attachment theory for psychiatry was John Bowlby, a British psychiatrist who worked at the Tavistock Clinic in London from the 1950s through the 1980s. Between 1969 and 1980, Bowlby published three volumes on attachment, separation, and loss (Bowlby, 1969, 1973, 1980). These writings are the foundation for the following overview of attachment behavior. In a recent review, Rutter concluded that empirical support exists for all of the key features of Bowlby's concepts (Rutter, 1995).

☐ Attachment Behavior

Bowlby defines attachment behavior as "any form of behavior that results in a person attaining or retaining proximity to some other differentiated and preferred individual, who is usually conceived as stronger and/or wiser" (Bowlby, 1977 p. 203). He identifies several signaling and approaching behaviors such as crying, non-nutritional sucking, smiling, touching, following, and calling that mediate attachment (Bowlby, 1969). Depending on the circumstances these attachment behaviors are associated with feelings of joy and love or anxiety and sorrow, with associated anger and protest (Bowlby, 1969, Bowlby, 1973). One of the most important insights of attachment theory is the proposition that attachment behavior is a primary drive system and an aggregation of brain functions that confer evolutionary advantage to the individual of a species. Attachment behavior serves as a protection against predators through maintaining a relationship to parents and membership in social groups (Bowlby, 1969).

As a corollary of the view that attachment behavior provides an evolutionary edge for survival, isolation from attachment figures is a situation that is threatening in the perspective of evolution. Attachment behavior stimulated by isolation is accompanied by strong feelings of alarm, anxiety, anger, loneliness, and insecurity (Bowlby, 1969). What is unique about this view is the idea that the absence of an attachment figure can stimulate fear just as strongly and surely as the presence of a frightening stimulus, such as a threatening situation, person, or predator (Bowlby, 1973). In the circumstances of separation and loss, humans experience separation anxiety as an essential part of the reaction that we recognize as grief. A knowledge of normal separation anxiety provides a cornerstone for understanding Traumatic Grief and developing criteria for its diagnosis. Because of its importance for the purposes of this book, separation anxiety is defined and discussed below.

Attachment behaviors are conspicuous in infants and young children in the circumstances of separation from their mothers. In response to the

"Strange Situation" procedure employed in studying infants, attachment behavior can be classified into four main types: secure, avoidant, resistant-ambivalent, and disorganized-disoriented (Ainsworth, Biehar, Waters, Wall, 1978; Main & Solomon, 1990). The activation of attachment behavior begins to attenuate in puberty. Still, although attachment behavior is less readily activated in adults, a propensity persists throughout adult life to monitor the environment for attachment figures and seek them out in times of stress. Progressively, investigators have characterized attachment styles in adults that are related to those in infants and probably related to psychopathology in adults (Main, 1996). The strongest and most common stimuli that evoke acute attachment behavior in adults are serious illnesses affecting the self and family members and losses of intimate relationships (Bowlby, 1977; Bowlby, 1980). In adult life, these stimuli arouse attachment behavior that we recognize as grief, including, as one component, separation anxiety. In the absence of losses, attachment behavior in adults is difficult to discern in everyday life as each person's unique nature mixes with nuturant experience and simple behavior patterns from childhood become overlaid with compensatory behavioral mechanisms.

Individuals vary in their susceptibility to fear in situations that might evoke separation anxiety (Bowlby, 1973). Early experiences with caregivers and an individual's temperament contribute to the development of attachment styles that persist into adulthood. Attachment styles, particularly anxious forms of attachment, interact with the actualities of current circumstances to determine the occurrence of maladaptive attachment behavior in adults. In addition, separation, loss, and insecure attachment probably predispose to childhood and adult psychiatric disorders (see the section on attachment behavior and psychopathology).

Before discussing the psychobiology of attachment, it is worth noting that attachment theory makes it possible to attempt an answer to the question of why humans grieve after the death of an intimate, an event in a person's life that is inevitable and irrevocable. The point is that attachment behavior, in this case grief, is a fundamental drive and biologic process evoked by a death. Grief is an expression of the drive to maintain the bond to the deceased person and protect the individual (in an evolutionary sense), no matter how painful, unrealistic, and dysfunctional it may be in a particular situation (Bowlby, 1980). In a sense, it is a vestige of behavior that is more fully developed and functional for the preservation of the species at an early stage of development but serves little functional purpose, or at best is a two edged sword, among adults. Indeed, intense and maladaptive attachment behavior in adults may place them at risk for psychiatric illnesses.

☐   **Neurobiology of Affiliation**

For the Adolf Meyer Lecture of the 135th Meeting of the American Psychiatric Association, MacLean posited that the phylogenetically latest division of the limbic system and the prefrontal cortex, which distinguish mammals and the human brain from other, more primitive, reptilian and amphibian species, developed in concert with the emergence of maternal care, play, the isolation call, and altruism (MacLean, 1990). As evolution conferred advantage to social bonding, brain structures emerged as substrates for affiliative behavior.

Coincident with the development of attachment theory and perhaps spurred in part by attachment theory, there is burgeoning knowledge of the biology and neural substrates of affiliation (Reite and Field, 1985; Carter et al., 1997). Affiliation refers to social behaviors that bring individuals closer together including such forms of positive association as attachment, parent-offspring interactions, pair-bonding, and coalitions (Carter et al., 1997). Affiliations provide a social matrix for reproduction and aggressive behavior. Since 1990, studies of affiliation have increased ten fold, while studies of aggression have declined somewhat, perhaps reflecting the growing acceptance that affiliative behaviors are related to primary drives and are not derivatives of sexual and aggressive behavior (Carter, 1997).

The neuroanatomical areas involved in affiliative behavior include the hypothalamus and limbic systems, which may regulate social approach and avoidance. Specifically, studies implicate systems based in the medial amygdala in avoidance, while those systems integrated by the medial preoptic area and ventral portion of the bed nucleus of the stria terminalis may regulate social approach. Approach is activated and avoidance inhibited for affiliative behavior to occur (Keverne, Nevison, & Martel, 1997). In addition, an evolutionary later system of the vagal nerve is involved in regulating complex social behavior including facial expression (Porges, 1997). Analysis of mechanisms focus on several neuropeptides including the endogenous opiates, oxytocin, vasopressin, the steroid hormones of the adrenal axis, the central nervous system amine systems, and the hypophysio-pituitary adrenal axis (Carter et al., 1997; Porges, 1997; Levine, Lyons, & Schatzberg, 1997).

In mammals, there is an increase in the role of cognition in the control of affiliative behavior in addition to the emotional and hormonal systems exerting control in other animals (Keverne et al., 1997; Snowdon, 1997). Consequently, there is growing appreciation that the organization of the cognitive, hormonal, and emotional systems that regulate social behavior depend on early caregiver-infant attachment rather than developing as an autonomous biological process (Kraemer, 1997). Indeed, not only social behavior but also personal homeostasis is served by relationships, originally with primary attachment figures such as the mother (Hofer, 1984). If these ideas continue to prove true in subsequent research, this may be an example of how the ontogeny of the affiliative, neurobiologic systems, although emerging from a complex interplay of nature and nurture, recapitulates the phylogeny of MacLean's thesis about evolution of the human brain (MacLean, 1990).

This brief summary is neither a thorough nor critical review of the neurobiology of affiliation or attachment. Rather, it is intended to indicate the enormous interest that now exists and the development of knowledge about how the brain is organized and how it functions to accomplish attachment behaviors. Progressively and perhaps incrementally over the next few years, neurobiologic research in animals that exhibit attachment behavior will inform our understanding of human attachment behavior.

Before leaving this overview of the neurobiology of affiliation, let me make a final note about a byproduct of the new technology for brain imaging. Posatron Emission Tomography scans now provide images of those regions of the human brain activated by test induced feelings of loss. Consistent with the discussion above, these studies identify diffuse limbic and prefrontal areas as the loci of these emotions (Pardo, Pardo, & Raichle, 1991; George et al., 1995).

☐ Separation Anxiety After a Loss

Bowlby never precisely defined separation anxiety. At one point, in concurring with later Freudian theory of anxiety, he wrote "separation anxiety is the reaction to the danger of losing the object" (Bowlby, 1973, p. 29). At another point, in the midst of a metaphor about an army in the field with a commander-in-chief dependent not only on defending the army against direct attack but also "on maintaining open communications with its base," Bowlby characterized separation anxiety as the reaction of the commander "when lines of communication with base are in jeopardy" (Bowlby, 1973, p. 94). More succinctly perhaps, Parkes defined separation anxiety as "the subjective accompaniment of awareness of the danger of loss" (Parkes, 1969, p. 87).

As noted previously, humans experience separation anxiety in the circumstances of separation and loss. Most commonly and conspicuously, adults experience separation anxiety after the death of an intimate. Separation anxiety occasioned by a death is made up of two components: the pang of grief and searching behavior. After a death, the acutely bereaved person experiences waves of episodic distress that Lindeman first described as the pangs of grief (Lindeman, 1944). These are self-limited episodes and characterized by intense yearning for the person who is lost. In addition, there are preoccupations with past experiences, crying, sighing, and a perceptual set for the lost person including dreams, tactile, visual and auditory illusions, and sometimes, frank hallucinations (Parkes, 1969).

The behavioral counterpart of pining is searching for the deceased person through seeking out places and things identified with that person, as if for the sake of regaining what has been lost (Bowlby & Parkes, 1970). For many bereaved persons there is a hypervigilant quality to the searching as they search the environment for cues of the lost person (Raphael and Martinek, 1997). In the circumstances of a death, searching behavior, which is often nonverbal and unconscious, inevitably ends in frustration. Typically, the frustration triggers another pang of grief.

Protest over separation is typical among children separated from attachment figures (Bowlby, 1973). It is less conspicuous in adults than in children. Nevertheless, it can be observed in adults in confrontations or conflicts with authority figures, particularly the physician, after a death occurs. Sometimes, the complaints of surviving family about medical care during a terminal illness of a family member are justified; sometimes the complaints are based on ignorance of the complexity of medical treatment; sometimes there appears to be little justification for the complaints. In all these instances, there is usually some admixture of protest. In some cases, the protest is directed towards religious authority and can result in estrangement from long held beliefs and practices. This alienation usually stems from feelings about the unfairness of the loss or disappointment with the response of religious figures to the needs of the bereaved person after the death. Protest goes hand in glove with separation anxiety and is rooted in the insecurity caused by the death.

A brief note on terminology is necessary before proceeding. In 1983, Raphael introduced the terms "separation pain" and "separation distress" to denote separation anxiety as defined by Bowlby and Parkes (Raphael, 1983). Separation distress seemed to describe better the phenomena in adults during bereavement, when typical manifestations of somatic anxiety are not conspicuous. Also, use of the term "separation distress" sidestepped theoretical connotations and disputes associated with the term "separation anxiety" as well as not connoting something psychopathologic or undesirable. After all, separation distress is quite normal and becomes part of a morbid picture only in the minority of cases. Therefore, I chose to use the term "separation distress" (Jacobs, 1993). In the meantime, there is growing acceptance of the concept of separation anxiety and even Separation Anxiety Disorders in adults, in reference to similar phenomena in children (see chapter 2). In addition, perhaps the term "separation anxiety" preserves more clearly the relationship among attachment theory, neurobiologic studies, children, and adults. Therefore, I find myself reverting to the term "separation anxiety" in some discussions. I will use "separation anxiety" and "separation distress" interchangeably. While both refer to the basic phenomena defined above, I tend to use the former term in theoretical discussions and the latter in clinical discussions of adult disorders.

☐ An Example of Separation Anxiety

Mrs. A.

Mrs. A. presented for evaluation 10 months after the sudden, unexpected death of her 24-year-old son from an acute brain disease and 7 months after the death of her mother from cancer. In part, she was suffering from bereavement overload from the double losses. She had not grieved after the death of her son and had redoubled her efforts to care for her terminally ill mother. When her mother died her grief hit her and she could not stop crying. Her chief complaint was "I can't believe it; it is such a shock." She was obsessed with the details of her son's death, as if she could undo them, and she wanted him back. She yearned intensely for the return of both her son and mother. She could think of little else and was annoyed by distractions from this preoccupation. These feelings were accompanied by crying and occurred episodically throughout the day. They were often precipitated by empty situations or unexpected reminders, and lasted 20–30 minutes. Her performance at work and her relationship with her family suffered which provided the main impetus for her seeking help. She came for evaluation under pressure from her family and remained avoidant for treatment tasks that focused on the losses for the first 3 meetings I had with her. She was compulsively drawn to visit the cemetery where her son was buried and was fighting this impulse as irrational. She also sought solace in a public park that she frequented with her adult children on holidays, as if she might be reunited with him there. She said she felt as if "part of me was gone." She felt useless to herself and others, especially her surviving children and her deceased son, whom she felt she had failed. She had no interest in or hopes for a meaningful future. She feared the sorrow over her losses was so intense it would drive her crazy. She was concerned about a change in her personality reflecting vague cognitive difficulties she was having. After repeated careful mental status exams, this was seen as an identification symptom related to personality changes in her son during his final weeks of life before dying from an acute brain disease. She had lost her sense of security, no longer trusted a capricious world, as she viewed it, and felt she had lost control over her life, which had been largely tied up in being an efficacious mother. Her anger and irritability, which was somewhat associated with protest over her fate and dissatisfaction with the doctors who were late in diagnosing her son, interfered with her relationships to her surviving children and her husband. These symptoms and problems had persisted for 7 months without significant improvement and the anniversary of her son's death loomed as a nemesis for her.

This bereaved mother illustrated the experience of severe separation anxiety reflected in a fear that she would be driven crazy. The separation anxiety was characterized by intense yearning, preoccupations, and the impulse to search for her son at the cemetery and in other places. Incidentally, she met criteria for the diagnosis of Traumatic Grief, including 3 of the criteria under Criterion A and 8 of the criteria under Criterion B, as well as Criteria C and D (see chapters 2 and 3).

☐   Separation Anxiety and Normal Grief

While separation anxiety is the nucleus it is not the whole picture of grief as we have come to understand it over the past 50 years. Starting with Lindeman's classic description, several authors have augmented our understanding of the phenomenology of grief (Lindeman, 1944; Parkes, 1970; Clayton, Desmarais, Winokur, 1968; Clayton, Halikas, & Maurice, 1971; Jacobs, Kasl, Ostfeld, Berkman, & Charpentier, 1986a; Jacobs et al., 1986b; Jacobs et al., 1987; Shuchter, 1986; Sanders, 1989; Shuchter & Zisook, 1993). The manifestations of grief are manifold. They include emotional numbness, disbelief, longing, yearning for the lost person, preoccupations with the deceased person, sighing, crying, dreams, illusions, hallucinations, seeking out places and things associated with the deceased person, irritability, anger, protest, sadness, depressed mood, anxiety, despair, insomnia, anorexia, fatigue, lethargy, guilt, loss of interest in usual activities, disorganization of behavior patterns that used to be related to the deceased person, and vague somatic symptoms. Typically, these manifestations peak in intensity in the first few months of bereavement and subside over the first year, though grief is still moderately intense for many people one year after the death.

Attachment theory helps organize this long list of manifestations. A model of grief as a multidimensional process (see Table 1) that evolves over time is more realistic and accurate than a model of several stages of

TABLE 1. Manifestations of Grief

Manifestations	Aggregations	Dimensions
Yearning	Pangs	Separation
Preoccupations		distress
Sighing		(anxiety)
Crying		
Illusions	Searching	
Dreams		
Hallucinations		
Searching		
Anger	Protest	
Protest		
Arousal	Anxious mood	
Anxiety/panic		
Sadness	Depressive mood	Mourning
Nostalgia		
Despair		
Insomnia	Neurovegetative	
Anorexia	Symptoms	
Fatigue		
Lethargy		
Loss of interests		
Loss of meaning	Disorganization	
Aimless behavior		
Numbness	Avoidance	Traumatic
Disbelief		distress
Horrific images	Intrusion	
Nightmares		
Somatic symptoms		Ailments
Coping behavior		Recovery
Attenuating distress		
Acceptance		
Remembering		
New commitments		

grief, which is often used as a Procrustean bed that is imposed on bereaved individuals. Within a multidimensional model, although all dimensions are present simultaneously, one dimension might predominate at a particular point in time leading to the appearance of stages and accounting for that perception. The concept of separation anxiety is a nucleus for understanding normal grief, however, depression/mourning and trauma/dissociative groups of symptoms, as well as coping processes and recovery also contribute to a complete picture.

Even if separation anxiety is only one of multiple dimensions of normal grief, it is arguable that it is an essential component of grief and more important than any other. Either excessive separation anxiety or the absence of it is a good indication of an aberrant pattern of grief. In short, separation anxiety provides a cornerstone for defining and thinking about Traumatic Grief.

☐ Attachment Behavior and Psychopathology

A person's early experience with caregivers and individual temperament integrate to establish attachment behaviors in infants. These persist into adulthood as attachment styles. The outcome can be secure adult attachment or insecure, anxious attachment. Anxious attachment includes both resistant-ambivalent and avoidant variants (Bowlby, 1973; Bowlby, 1977; Bowlby, 1988; Ainsworth et al., 1978). A fourth attachment styled called disorganized-disoriented also occurs (Main & Solomon, 1990). The relationship of these attachment styles to Axis II personality diagnoses is obscure at the present time.

It is reasonable to hypothesize that insecure attachment styles in adults become exaggerated and perhaps maladaptive in circumstances where primary attachments are threatened or lost. Paradoxically, the same attachment behaviors that enhance survival for infants by ensuring proximity to a caretaker may not operate for good and obvious reasons for some adults. Some attachment behaviors may even put them at risk such as when the drive to be close to or reunited with an attachment figure is experienced at the same level of intensity as that experienced by the young. According to Bowlby's later views, cognitive biases about attachment figures, developed through predisposition to form anxious attachments and early experiences such as partial or intermittent rejection by parents, lay a groundwork for absent and chronic grief or, in other words, pathologic grief.

Furthermore, Bowlby notes that insecure attachment predisposes to school phobias (Separation Anxiety Disorder) in children. Also, according to Bowlby, children with Separation Anxiety Disorder bear a close resemblance to adults with agoraphobia and panic attacks (Bowlby, 1973, 1980). DSM-IV defines separation anxiety and the occurrence of Separation Anxiety Disorder exclusively in terms related to children (DSM-IV, 1994). In part because the manual does not acknowledge a Separation Anxiety Disorder in adults, it says nothing about separation anxiety in adults in the circumstances of a death.

Current psychiatric investigators, particularly in the field of developmental psychology, have pursued the study of the relationship between attachment behavior and psychopathology in a concerted way for the past several years (del Carmen & Huffman, 1996). The development of the Adult Attachment Interview (George et al., 1996) has spurred new studies of adolescent and adult attachment representations and styles and their relationships to psychopathology. In current research, investigators using primarily case control, cross sectional designs in both patient and nonpatient samples, are exploring associations of attachment behavior with a variety of psychopathology (Fonagy et al., 1996; Rosenstein & Horowitz, 1996; Allen, Hauser, & Borman-Spurrell, 1996; Adam, Sheldon-Keller, & West, 1996; Pianta, Egeland, & Adam, 1996; Cole-Detke & Kobak, 1996). The types of psychopathology include affective disorders, anxiety disorders, severe personality disorders, eating disorders, drug use, and suicidal behavior. There is some preliminary evidence that specific attachment styles are associated with specific disorders and some evidence that certain, insecure attachment styles are associated with a high risk of psychopathology of various types. Judging from these studies, it would seem that the complex relationship between attachment behavior and psychopathology will become progressively clearer as this new focus of research develops.

☐ Conclusion

Evolution theory and Darwin's observations on emotions in several animal species opened up new perspectives on human grief. These new vistas are embodied largely in attachment theory. Attachment theory and knowledge of attachment behaviors provide a framework not only for thinking about normal grief but also the clinical complications of bereavement. In particular, I believe the concept of separation anxiety is a starting point that is necessary but not sufficient for conceptualizing Traumatic Grief. Indeed, other emotional states associated with grief such as depressive mood or traumatic distress have served as additional stepping stones to understanding adult psychopathology in the circumstances of bereavement. Ethology and attachment theory have led to a blossoming of neurobiologic studies of affiliation, including attachment behaviors as a primary set of behaviors in their own right, independent of and interactive with sexual and aggressive behaviors.

One of the challenges for clinicians concerned with the clinical complications of bereavement is the task of making a diagnosis and making decisions about diagnosis and treatment during the process of normal grief. Knowledge of attachment behavior, the neurobiology of attachment, and normal grief is an essential for diagnostic thinking about Traumatic Grief and its treatment with the consensus diagnostic criteria that are presented in chapter 2.

☐ References

Adam, K. S., Sheldon-Keller, A. E., West, M. (1996). Attachment organization and history of suicidal behavior in clinical adolescents. *Journal of Consulting and Clinical Psychology, 64,* 264–272.

Ainsworth, M. D. S., Biehar, M. C., Waters, E., & Wall, S. Eds. (1978). Patterns of attachment: A psychological study of the strange situation. Hillsdale, NJ: Erlbaum Publishing.

Allen, J. P., Hauser, S. T., & Borman-Spurrell, E. (1996). Attachment theory as a framework for understanding sequellae of severe adolescent psychopathology: An 11 year follow-up study. *Journal of Consulting and Clinical Psychology, 64,* 254–263.

Bowlby, J. (1969). *Attachment and loss, vol 1: Attachment.* New York: Basic Books.

Bowlby, J. (1973). *Attachment and loss, vol 2: Separation.* New York: Basic Books.

Bowlby, J. (1977). The making and breaking of affectional bonds. *British Journal of Psychiatry, 130,* 201–210.

Bowlby, J. (1980). *Attachment and loss, volume 3: Loss, sadness and depression.* New York: Basic Books.

Bowlby, J. (1988). Developmental psychiatry comes of age. *The American Journal of Psychiatry, 145,* 1–10.

Bowlby, J., & Parkes, C. M. (1970). Separation and loss within the family. In E. J. Anthony and C. M. Koupernil (Eds.), *International yearbook for child psychiatry and allied disciplines, vol 1: The child in his family.* (pp. 197–216. New York: Wiley.

Carter, C. S., Lederhendler, I. I., & Kirkpatrick, B. (1997). Introduction. *Annals of the New York Academy of Sciences, 807,* xiii–xvii.

Clayton, P. J., Desmarais, L., & Winokur, G. (1968). A study of normal bereavement. *American Journal of Psychiatry, 125,* 168–178.

Clayton, P. J., Halikas, J. A., & Maurice, W. L. (1971). The bereavement of the widowed. *Diseases of the Nervous System, 32,* 597–604.

Cole-Detke, H., & Hobak, R. (1996). Attachment processes in eating disorder and depression. *Journal of Consulting and Clinical Psychology, 64,* 282–290.

Darwin, C. (1872). *The expression of the emotions in man and animals.* London: John Murray.

del Carmen, R., Huffman, L. (1996). Epilogue: Bridging the gap between research on attachment and psychopathology. *Journal of Consulting and Clinical Psychology, 64,* 292–294.

Diagnostic and Statistical Manual of Mental Disorders (4th ed.). (1994). Washington, DC: American Psychiatric Press, Inc.

Fonagy, P., Leigh, T., Steele, M., Steele, H., Kennedy, R., Mattoon, G., Target, M., & Gerber, A. (1996). The relation of attachment status, psychiatric classification, and response to psychotherapy. *Journal of Consulting and Clinical Psychology, 64,* 22–31.

George, C., Kaplan, N., & Main, M. Adult attachment interview. Unpublished protocol, Department of Psychology, University of California, Berkeley, CA.

George, M. S., Ketter, T. A., Parekh, P. I., Horwitz, B., Herscovitch P., & Post, R. W. (1998). Regional brain activity of 11 healthy women during sadness. *American Journal of Psychiatry, 152,* 341–351.

Hofer, M. A. (1984). Relationships as regulators: A psychobiologic perspective on bereavement. *Psychosomatic Medicine, 46,* 183–197.

Jacobs, S. C., Kasl, S. V., Ostfeld, A. M., Berkman, L., & Charpentier, P. (1986a). The measurement of grief: Age and sex variation. *British Journal of Medical Psychology, 59,* 305–310.

Jacobs, S. C., Kasl, S. V., Ostfeld, A. M., Berkman, L., Kosten, T. R., & Charpentier, P. (1986b). The measurement of grief: Bereaved versus nonbereaved. *The Hospice Journal, 2,* 21–36.

Jacobs, S. C., Kosten, T. R., Kasl, S. V., Ostfeld, A. M., Berkman, L., & Charpentier, P. (1981). Attachment theory and multiple and multiple dimensions of grief. *Omega, 18*, 41–52.

Jacobs, S. (1993). *Pathologic grief: Maladaptation to loss.* Washington, DC: American Psychiatric Press.

Keverne, E. B., Nevison, C. M., & Martel, F. L. (1997). Early learning and the social bond. *Annals of the New York Academy of Sciences, 807*, 329–339.

Kraemer, G. W. (1997). Psychobiology of early social attachment in Rhesus monkeys: Clinical implications. *Annals of the New York Academy of Sciences, 807*, 401–418.

Levine, S., Lyons, D. M., & Schatzberg, A. F. (1997). Psychobiological consequences of social relationships. *Annals of the New York Academy of Sciences, 807*, 210–218.

Lindeman, E. (1944). Symptomatology and management of acute grief. *American Journal of Psychiatry, 101*, 141–148.

MacLean, P. D. (1990). *The triune brain in evolution.* New York: Plenum Press.

Main, M., & Solomon, J. (1990). Procedures for identifying infants as disorganized/disoriented during the Ainsworth strange situation. In M. T. Greenberg, D. Cicchetti, & E. M. Cummings (Eds.), *Attachment in the preschool years* (p. 87). Chicago: University of Chicago Press.

Main, M. (1996). Introduction to the special section on attachment and psychopathology: 2. Overview of the field of attachment. *Journal of Consulting and Clinical Psychology, 264*, 237–243.

Pardo, J. V., Pardo, P. J., & Raichle, M. E. (1991). Neural correlates of dysphoria. *American Journal of Psychiatry, 150*, 713–719.

Parkes, C. M. (1969). Separation anxiety: An aspect of the search for a lost object. In M. H. Lader, (Ed.), *Studies of Anxiety.* British Journal of Psychiatry, special publication #3.

Parkes, C. M. (1970). The first year of bereavement: A longitudinal study of the reaction of London widows to the death of their husbands. *Psychiatry, 33*, 449–467.

Pianta, R. C., Egeland, B., & Adam, E. K. (1996). Adult attachment classification and self-reported psychiatric symptomatology as assessed by the MMPI-2. *Journal of Consulting and Clinical Psychology, 64*, 273–281.

Porges, S. W. (1997). Emotion: An evolutionary by-product of the neural regulation of the autonomic nervous system. *Annals of the New York Academy of Sciences, 807*, 62–77.

Raphael, B. (1983). *The anatomy of bereavement.* New York: Basic Books.

Raphael, B., & Martinek, N. (1997). Assessing traumatic bereavement and post traumatic stress disorder. In J. P. Wilson, & T. M. Keane, (Eds.), (pp. 373–395). New York: The Guilford Press.

Reite, M., & Field, T. (Eds.). (1985). *The psychobiology of attachment and separation.* New York: Academic Press.

Rosenstein, D. S., & Horowitz, H. A. (1996). Adolescent attachment and psychopathology. *Journal of Consulting and Clinical Psychology, 64*, 244–253.

Rutter, M. (1995). Clinical implications of attachment concepts: Retrospect and prospect. *Journal of Child Psychology and Psychiatry, 36*, 549–571.

Sanders, C. M. (1989). *Grief: The mourning after.* New York: John Wiley and Sons.

Shuchter, S. R. (1986). *The dimensions of grief: Adjusting to the death of a spouse.* San Francisco: Jossey-Bass Publishers.

Shuchter, S. R., & Zisook, S. (1993). The course of normal grief. In M. S. Stroebe, W. Stroebe, & R. O. Hansson (Eds.), *Handbook of bereavement: Theory, research, and intervention* (pp. 23–43). Cambridge, England: Cambridge University Press.

Snowdon, C. T. (1997). Affiliative processes and vocal development. *Annals of the New York Academy of Sciences, 807*, 340–351.

Definition of Traumatic Grief as a Disorder

☐ The Concept of Pathologic Grief

In many respects, the development of the concept of "pathologic grief" is a 20th century project starting with the publication of *Mourning and Melancholia* by Freud in 1917 (Freud, 1953). Based on clinical observations from psychoanalysis, Freud asserted that depressive illness (melancholia) occurred during bereavement in circumstances where the relationship to the deceased was narcissistic and ambivalent. During grief, the bereaved person destined to develop melancholia introjects attributes of the lost person, and, at the same time, anger at the deceased person for abandoning him or her is turned against the self. While this is a psychologic dynamic that clinicians can observe in a minority of cases, perhaps the most enduring legacy of Freud's thesis is a continuing assumption in many clinicians' minds of a close relationship, if not a continuum, between grief and depression. According to this view, if grief were to take a pathologic turn, it would manifest as a major depressive episode. Perhaps, Clayton's studies of major depressive illness as a clinical complication of bereavement are a reflection of this view (Clayton, 1990).

While there is evidence for a higher risk of Major Depressions during acute bereavement (see the citations in the Preface), there is also evidence for a higher risk of anxiety disorders and Post-traumatic Stress Disorder. Post-traumatic Stress Disorder is more likely to occur if the death is violent, sudden, or unexpected. Recognition of these disorders also provides a useful perspective on the clinical complications of bereavement and serves as a basis for a discussion of comorbidity in chapter 4. For the purposes of presenting working diagnostic criteria for Traumatic Grief, I want to focus on two other, main currents in 20th century writing on the clinical complications of bereavement. One stems from Lindeman through Bowlby and Parkes and leads to a concept of "pathologic grief" rooted in attachment behavior. The other current stems from Adler through Horowitz and offers a view of "pathologic grief" as a type of trauma or stress related disorder.

In 1944, Lindeman, writing about bereaved persons seeking help in the aftermath of the Coconut Grove fire in Boston, first characterized the pang of grief. In characterizing the pang of grief, he described the unbidden, episodic occurrence of intense pining for the deceased person, preoccupation with the loss, crying, and sighing (Lindeman, 1944). Intense pangs of grief could become part of a larger picture of pathologic grief, which in Lindeman's view also included somatic symptoms, guilt, hostile reactions, and loss of patterns of conduct. Subsequently, Bowlby built on this seminal description of pathologic grief with his concept of separation anxiety (see chapter 1). Parkes, another British psychiatrist who worked contemporaneously with Bowlby, carried out much of the empirical work in bereaved adults that supported the idea that separation distress is a cornerstone of normal grief (Parkes, 1972). Each of them contributed to a typology of a disorder of bereavement using manifestations of separation anxiety as a foundation. In his later writing, Bowlby referred to two presentations of complicated bereavement. One was chronic grief, and the other was essentially absent grief (Bowlby, 1980). Parkes, based on his empirical studies of bereaved adults, refined those two categories into three: inhibited grief (i.e., absent or minimal), delayed grief, which was characterized by late onset and was typically intense, and prolonged, chronic grief (Parkes, 1965).

It is not widely appreciated that Adler, making observations at the Boston City Hospital emergency room of bereaved survivors of the Coconut Grove fire in parallel with Lindeman at Massachusetts General Hospital, was the first person to relate the psychiatric complications of the disaster not only to the deaths but also to the traumatic circumstances of the fire (Adler, 1943). In her view, the trauma was the most salient aspect of the problem, leading her to characterize the clinical problems she encountered as anxiety neuroses, with symptoms similar to Post-traumatic Stress Disorders.

In the 1970s, Horowitz began a series of studies of complicated bereavement as a stress related disorder that carried forward the earlier observations by Adler that a disorder of bereavement can be rooted in traumatic aspects of a death (Horowitz, 1976). He contributed to our understanding of traumatic distress by, among other things, conceptualizing two aspects of the turmoil. One aspect was intrusive symptoms, including frightening perceptions, hypervigilance, startle reactions, feelings of helplessness, and insecurity. The other aspect was avoidant and psychologically self-protective symptoms, including denial, dissociation, and aversion to painful reminders. On a descriptive level, Horowitz developed a scale for assessment of traumatic phenomena (Horowitz, Wilner, & Alvarez, 1979). The Impact of Events Scale included two subscales. One, the avoidance subscale, included eight items that assessed behavioral avoidance and emotional numbing. The other, the intrusion subscale, included seven items that ambiguously refer to separation anxiety. The intrusive, episodic qualities of these items are similar to the pang of grief. Recently, Horowitz and colleagues introduced criteria for Complicated Grief Disorder based on his concepts (Horowitz et al., 1997). These will be discussed later in the chapter in a comparison of the two published criteria sets.

Recently, investigators with considerable experience in both the fields of bereavement and trauma have usefully drawn a contrast between grief and traumatic distress for both adults and children (Pynoos & Nader, 1990; Raphael & Martinek, 1997; Nader, 1997). In particular, Raphael, a long standing leader in the field of bereavement and trauma studies, dissects the phenomena of grief and trauma, delineates the distinctions in the cognitive, affective, avoidant, and arousal symptoms, and presents them in a series of tables. In summary, the bereaved person with separation distress is preoccupied with the deceased person, seeks for reminders of the dead person, and is aroused and focused on the lost person. In contrast, the traumatized person is preoccupied with the scene of the trauma and the violent encounter with death, wishes to avoid reminders of the event, and is hypervigilantly aroused and oriented to threat, danger, or the return of a similar threat. By defining the phenomena clearly, Raphael helps us to understand the differences and sets the stage for thinking about a potential integration of the two fields of thanatology and trauma, an undertaking that leading therapists and clinical investigators have recently called for (Rando, 1993; Figley, Bride, & Mazza, 1997).

Beginning with Lindeman and Adler, who worked in parallel and apparently in isolation of each other in the same city with survivors of the same fire, there has been a lag in the integration of their two perspectives on a disorder of bereavement. A consensus conference convened recently at the Department of Psychiatry of the University of Pittsburgh brought experts from both points of view together to see if they could agree on a common set of diagnostic criteria that would reconcile these two different streams of development (Prigerson et al., in press; Prigerson & Jacobs, in press). The conference utilized recent empirical work by Prigerson and colleagues as a starting point for discussion. Prigerson's studies have been successful in identifying a single domain of symptoms, unifying the two historical perspectives on separation anxiety and traumatic distress, and verifying the construct of a disorder incorporating these symptoms according to established validation strategies incorporated into the Diagnostic and Statistical Manual (Guze, 1970).

☐ Consensus Diagnostic Criteria for Traumatic Grief

For the sake of clarity and consistency, it is useful to describe first the choice of name for this disorder that occurs during bereavement. The name choice actually resulted from review of data and a process of consensus building at the conference described below (Prigerson, Maciejewski, Pilkonis, Wortman, Williams, Widiger, Davidson, Frank, Kupfer, Zisook, in press; Prigerson & Jacobs, in press). In other words, it came at the end of a process and in reverse order of the way I am presenting it here. Although, many in the group had referred to the disorder as complicated grief in previous publications, the conference panel agreed on the name "Traumatic Grief" for several reasons. First, the name Traumatic Grief avoids confusion with previous terms such as pathologic, neurotic, or morbid grief, which have negative connotations. Also, Traumatic Grief is preferable to the terms complicated or unresolved grief, which are vague or narrow in meaning. Traumatic Grief more concretely and precisely captures the two underlying dimensions of the disorder, that is, separation distress and traumatic distress, two distinctly delineated domains of distress (Raphael & Martinek, 1997). The word "traumatic" refers in the new terminology to the phenomenology of the disorder, not the etiology, as the disorder can occur in the absence of an objectively traumatic death as the discussion below on the kinds of losses that can serve as triggers will clarify. With this explanation completed, I'll describe the process of discussion at the consensus conference (Prigerson et al., in press; Prigerson & Jacobs, in press).

The consensus conference of experts began by addressing the question of whether there is a need to establish criteria for the diagnosis of Traumatic Grief (Prigerson & Jacobs, in press). There was unanimous agreement about the need for this development. In part, this decision was in response to multiple calls in the literature for diagnostic criteria for a disorder associated with bereavement (Horowitz et al., 1984; Horowitz, Bonannon, Holen, 1993; Kim & Jacobs, 1991; Prigerson et al., 1995a; Raphael & Middleton, 1990). The decision was also based on review of the following evidence.

In recent factor analyses of data from both clinical and community based samples, Prigerson and colleagues have found evidence of a unified factor that 1) incorporates elements of both separation distress and traumatic distress, 2) persists cohesively over several months and sometimes years, and 3) is distinct from both depressive and anxiety factors (Prigerson et al., 1995a; Prigerson et al., 1995b; Prigerson et al., 1996). Eventually, they referred to this syndrome as Traumatic Grief. Moreover, they replicated these results in men and women and in young adult, mid-life, and late-life clinical samples (see chapter 6).

As data suggesting that Traumatic Grief was a distinct syndrome emerged, evidence also mounted that Traumatic Grief is associated with present distress and disability, two basic criteria for qualifying as a disorder in the diagnostic manual (DSM-IV, 1994). For example, the items included in the Inventory of Complicated Grief (ICG), a scale derived from the factor analysis noted above, have face validity as distress. Also, Prigerson and colleagues demonstrated that Traumatic Grief assessed by the ICG six months after a loss is positively associated with subsequent assessments of impaired role performance, functional impairment, subjective sleep disturbance, low self-esteem, depression, and anxiety (Prigerson et al., 1995b). Moreover, they found that Traumatic Grief was associated with a high risk of cancer, cardiac disorders, alcohol and tobacco consumption, and suicidal ideation among older widows and widowers (Bierhals et al., 1995; Prigerson et al., 1997). Finally, in a study of young adults, those with high levels of Traumatic Grief symptoms had a greatly increased risk of suicidal ideation (Prigerson et al., in press).

While acknowledging that a wide range of manifestations and durations can be considered within normal limits, the panel of experts reached general agreement that marked levels of symptoms of Traumatic Grief lasting for more than 2 months were the cornerstone for developing criteria. It is now clear that marked symptoms pose significant risks for mental and physical morbidity, and this was a starting point for the discussion. In contrast, there was not consensus on the criterion of 2 months duration, and the consensus group emphasized a need for more empirical work. Some were concerned that a short duration criterion would encroach on the domain of normal bereavement responses. Still, there was agreement that initial reactions to loss often prove to be the best predictors of later difficulties. The panel worried that a longer criterion for duration would impose prolonged suffering on persons afflicted with the disorder and agreed that the benefits gained from early intervention outweighed the costs of treating a subset of individuals whose symptoms would resolve spontaneously. In addition, the 2 month criterion corresponded to the 2 month guideline in DSM for the diagnosis of Major Depressive Disorder in the circumstances of bereavement.

As a final task, the consensus experts considered what type of losses might serve as triggers for a disorder of bereavement. In the end, after pondering many types of losses that might cause a disorder, there was agreement to limit the type of loss to a death. The panel recommended that the criteria be defined in terms of any death of a significant other, whether objectively traumatic or not. The latter was not intended to suggest that a violent death or, for that matter, simply a sudden, unexpected death, might not cause a coexisting, diagnosable Post-traumatic Stress Disorder, particularly if there is direct exposure to horrifying aspects of the death. On the other hand, a nonviolent death might cause Traumatic Grief in a person with a strong predisposition. Aware that not all the questions in this area were supported by data, the panel of experts recognized the need for further research on what types of reactions occur after different types of losses.

For the purpose of diagnosis the panel concluded that, in addition to violent deaths with an obvious potential to be traumatic, the symptoms of Traumatic Grief can occur following any death that is personally devastating. In the latter case, the devastation can derive to some extent from a sudden, unexpected, and possibly untimely death but also from the quality of the relationship to the deceased or other personal predispositions. In short, the nucleus of Traumatic Grief was considered to be a traumatic separation that might have either developmental or environmental origins or both.

Thus, there are two potential pathways to the occurrence of the disorder that can amalgamate in particular cases. Through the developmental pathway attachment behaviors emerge in childhood resulting from a combination of inherited characteristics (such as temperament) and early developmental experiences. These attachment behaviors can persist into adulthood and predispose to a disorder in the circumstances of a death. Alternatively, a death can be inherently traumatic (violent, horrible, sudden, and unexpected) and fundamentally shake the assumptions about a secure life and future attachments of the bereaved survivor. In this circumstance, an attachment disorder can begin in adulthood and then continue into the future.

Through this consensus process the conference of experts recommended specific, diagnostic criteria for Traumatic Grief (Prigerson, in press; Prigerson & Jacobs, in press). The criteria are introduced here as part of the description of the development process. In chapter 3, I provide a more clinically oriented, concrete discussion of each criterion and how to use it in diagnosis. For our purposes here, the consensus conference proposed four criteria. Criterion A specifies that the symptoms of the disorder occur in the circumstances of the death of a significant other and include intrusive, distressing separation anxiety. Criterion B includes

11 symptoms that are indications of having been traumatized by the loss. Criterion C specifies that the duration of symptoms must be at least 2 months. Criterion D requires that the symptomatic disturbance causes clinically significant impairment in social, occupational, or other important areas of functioning.

These criteria need additional study and refinement to resolve important questions that the consensus panel was not able to answer with data. For example, empirical studies are needed to refine how many symptoms should be included under Criterion B, how many are required for diagnosis, and at what level of severity. Also, with working criteria such as the consensus set, more studies of the natural history of normal and traumatic grief leading to knowledge of factors that predict failure to spontaneously resolve normal grief, will be useful for determining who warrants diagnosis and treatment, and when. This will lead to refinement of Criterion C for the duration of the symptomatic disturbance. As a final example, investigation of variations in the typology of Traumatic Grief will resolve whether there are severe, chronic, and delayed subtypes, as the literature on pathologic grief suggests (Byrne & Raphael, 1994; Middleton, Raphael, Martinek, & Misso, 1993; Middleton, Burnett, Raphael, & Martinek, 1996; Raphael & Middleton, 1990; Parkes, 1970; Parkes & Weiss, 1983; Wortman & Silver, 1989; Zisook & Lyons, 1989).

☐ **Comparison of Criteria for Traumatic Grief With Another Set of Published Criteria**

Parallel with the studies of Prigerson and colleagues and the development of the consensus conference criteria for Traumatic Grief in Pittsburgh, Horowitz and colleagues have published criteria for Complicated Grief Disorder (Horowitz et al., 1997). They analyzed data from 70 voluntarily selected, bereaved persons who were evaluated 6 and 14 months after the death of a long term partner using latent class model analyses and signal detection procedures (Horowitz et al., 1997). Given the different theoretical orientations of the Horowitz group and the consensus panel of experts, the amount of agreement on criteria is impressive and provides encouraging validation of the process of developing criteria. Both sets of criteria emphasize interference or impairment in functioning. Both emphasize severe symptoms of separation distress, which Horowitz characterizes as intrusive, consistent with the nature of the pang of grief. Both include avoidance as a symptom, though this item does not perform well in either set of criteria as I will discuss in chapter 3. Both include loss of interest in usual pursuits. Finally, both include reference to feelings of emptiness and loneliness, although the latter item in the consensus set was a product of receiver operating characteristic analyses by Prigerson and colleagues subsequent to the consensus process.

There is a difference between the consensus criteria and Horowitz's criteria set for duration of symptoms. For Horowitz and colleagues, it is one month duration and at least 14 months after the death. The consensus criteria recommend 2 months duration without being defined in time relationship to the death. The consensus recommendation reflects a value placed on early intervention within the natural history of normal grief.

Also, each set includes some unique symptoms. The set for Complicated Grief Disorder includes interference with sleep, a symptom presumably reflecting hyperarousal. Sleep disturbance and other symptoms of hyperarousal were omitted from the consensus criteria because a sleep study has shown no evidence of hyperaroused sleep in Traumatic Grief and the subjective sleep disturbance in persons with Traumatic Grief is unrelated to the Traumatic Grief symptoms. In addition, the panel concluded that symptoms of hyperarousal are not prominent in these patients except for irritability, which was construed as part of anger and protest over the loss.

The consensus criteria include several symptoms under Criterion B that are not found in Horowitz's criteria set for Complicated Grief. These symptoms reflect the devastation in the bereaved person's life caused by the death. They include 1) detachment and absence of emotional responsiveness, 2) difficulty acknowledging the death (disbelief), 3) sense of futility, 4) difficulty imagining a fulfilling life, 5) feeling part of oneself has died, 6) harmful symptoms or behavior related to the deceased, and 7) a shattered world view. There were no closely related items in Horowitz's set of criteria with the exception of "emotional unavailability to others," which did not make it into his final set of criteria.

☐ Mental Disorders in DSM-IV and the Issue of Cultural Sanction

The template for the Traumatic Grief consensus group's work was the definition of mental disorders in DSM-IV. According to DSM-IV, a mental disorder is "a clinically significant behavioral or psychological syndrome or pattern that occurs in an individual and that is associated with present distress (e.g., a painful symptom) or disability (i.e., impairment in one or more areas of functioning) or with a significantly increased risk of suffering death, pain, disability, or an important loss of freedom."[14] (Diagnostic and Statistical Manual, Fourth Edition, 1994). DSM-IV continues to say,

"In addition, this syndrome or pattern must not be merely an expectable and culturally sanctioned response to a particular event, for example the death of a loved one. Whatever its cause, it must currently be considered a manifestation of a behavioral, psychological, or biological dysfunction in the individual" (DSM-IV 1994).

I believe that Traumatic Grief as presented in this chapter meets this definition. The issue of cultural sanction is a particularly thorny one for the diagnosis of Traumatic Grief which deserves emphasis and discussion. Based on the data summarized in this chapter, I argue that Traumatic Grief is not "merely an expectable and culturally sanctioned response to a particular event." Rather, for a minority of persons exposed to the death of a significant other and who develop a severe and prolonged course of disabling symptoms—those meet criteria for Traumatic Grief—the experience is an unexpected, undesirable "behavioral, psychological, or biological dysfunction in the individual." I believe that Traumatic Grief should not be culturally sanctioned as a normal response to a death but rather acknowledged as a disorder in a significant minority of bereaved persons. Furthermore, I believe that bereaved persons with Traumatic Grief will benefit from professional expertise in diagnosis and intervention with psychotherapy and psychotropic drugs.

I recognize that there is genuine concern about the development of diagnostic criteria for Traumatic Grief. To protect against over-diagnosis and harmful, albeit well meaning, intrusions of clinicians into the normal process of grief, I believe it is possible to strive for conservative diagnostic criteria giving low rates of false positives with a high degree of specificity in diagnosis. Also, professional attention to the disorder can be offered in a manner that is based on knowledge of normal grief and that is respectful to and does not damage natural, family, and social supports. In this way, it would be feasible to bring more help to those who suffer from Traumatic Grief without interfering with normal grief.

☐ The Nature of Traumatic Grief

As Traumatic Grief is a new diagnosis and empirical studies needed to elucidate its nature remain to be done, a discussion of the nature of the disorder is necessarily speculative. Nevertheless, it is helpful in thinking about Traumatic Grief as a disorder to put it in a context.

Traumatic Grief is distinct from other disorders by virtue of its unique diagnostic features rooted in the separation distress evoked by a death and certain aspects of traumatic distress. Still, Traumatic Grief has a generic relationship to Post-traumatic Stress Disorder and Acute Stress Disorder in the sense that they all occur after an event or experience in a person's life that opens a period of risk for the disorder.

A central question about the nature of Traumatic Grief is its relationship to Separation Anxiety Disorder in children. A case can be made for Traumatic Grief as an adult form of Separation Anxiety Disorder except that an adult form of Separation Anxiety Disorder is not accepted in current nomenclature and practice. Part of the problem is that the existing DSM-IV diagnostic criteria are strongly oriented to childhood experiences. Despite this obstacle, there is reason to press on with this comparison, given that marked and persistent separation distress, which occurs after a traumatic separation caused by a death, is a hallmark of Traumatic Grief.

It is interesting to note a few recent reports on Separation Anxiety Disorder in adults, one of which is a case report of successful treatment using behavior strategies for a childhood onset Separation Anxiety Disorder in an adult (Butcher, 1983). Another study reports on Separation Anxiety Disorder in young adults who leave home for college (Ollendick, Lease, & Cooper, 1993). After losses through death, it would seem that leaving home as a young adult is the circumstance that readily suggests itself as a place to look for such a disorder. A third study describes 3 cases of Separation Anxiety Disorder in adults (Manicavasagar & Silove, 1997). One is a young, immigrant woman whose symptoms intensified after arguments with her lover. Another is a young, immigrant man who could not tolerate separation from his wife and child, and another is a middle aged business man who had long standing anxiety about overseas travel and whose wife was being evaluated for gynecological cancer. The latter man gave no evidence of a disorder in childhood, while the other two did. The possibility of adult onset of Separation Anxiety Disorder, as in the last case, is consistent with the idea of two pathways to Traumatic Grief. In the case of an adult onset Separation Anxiety Disorder, a resilient personality could somehow carry a person through childhood. In the case of early onset in childhood, a strong predisposition would lead to earlier onset and should be reflected in evidence of childhood manifestations of Separation Anxiety Disorder, measured, for example, by the Separation Anxiety Symptom Inventory (Silove et al., 1993). There is now some preliminary interest in developing diagnostic criteria for adult Separation Anxiety Disorder (Shear, M. K., personal communication).

With this background, it is conceivable that adult Separation Anxiety Disorder is a nosologic concept that will develop more over the next few years. It is also conceivable that Traumatic Grief will ultimately be viewed as an adult form of Separation Anxiety Disorder and the name of the disorder might be changed accordingly.

Speculation on the nature of Traumatic Grief is useful for the purpose of providing ideas about where to look in the treatment literature for studies that are relevant for the disorder. Thus, if Traumatic Grief has a relationship to Separation Anxiety Disorder, it suggests the child psychiatry literature on treating Separation Anxiety Disorder may be relevant and provide important leads for treatment and studies of adults. Similarly, to the extent that there are traumatic elements in the syndrome, the treatment literature on Post-traumatic Stress Disorder can be explored for ideas. I use both these strategies in chapter 5.

☐ Conclusion and Definition of Traumatic Grief

The development of final criteria for diagnosis of Traumatic Grief is incomplete. The consensus criteria for Traumatic Grief require refinement through studies of their use in different samples and circumstances of death and in comparison to other criteria sets such as those of Horowitz and colleagues. In the meantime, they provide a sound basis for beginning to think diagnostically about Traumatic Grief.

This chapter has selectively reviewed the literature and described a consensus process that developed consensus criteria for Traumatic Grief. The process also contributed to a definition of Traumatic Grief. In summary, Traumatic Grief is a disorder that occurs after the death of a significant other. Symptoms of separation distress are the core of the disorder and amalgamate with bereavement specific symptoms of being devastated and traumatized by death. For diagnosis, the symptoms must be marked and persistent and last at least 2 months. The symptomatic disturbance causes clinically significant impairment in social, occupational, or other important areas of functioning. The use of "traumatic" in the name of the disorder does not refer to etiology but rather describes the phenomenology. Thus, the disorder may occur not only after deaths that are objectively violent and horrific but also in individuals who are highly vulnerable, after deaths that are not conspicuously traumatic. The nidus of the disorder for an individual is a traumatic separation. The disorder is one of a class of disorders, including Post-traumatic Stress Disorder and Acute Stress Disorder that occur after an event in a person's life which opens a period of risk for the disorder. Traumatic Grief may prove to be an adult form of Separation Anxiety Disorder; however considerable development of the concept of Separation Anxiety Disorder in adults and studies of Traumatic Grief as a new nosologic entity are necessary to establish this relationship.

☐ References

Adler, A. (1943). Neuropsychiatric complications in victims of Boston's Coconut Grove disaster. *Journal of the American Medical Association, 123*, 1098–1101.

Bierhals, A. J., Prigerson, H. G., Frank, E., Reynolds, C. F., Fasiczka, A., & Miller, M. D. (1995). Gender differences in complicated grief among the elderly. *Omega, 32*, 303–317.

Bowlby, J. (1980). *Attachment and loss, volume 3: Loss, sadness and depression.* New York: Basic Books.

Byrne, G., & Raphael, B. (1994). A longitudinal study of bereavement phenomena in recently widowed elderly men. *Psychological Medicine, 24*, 411–421.

Butcher, P. (1983). The treatment of childhood-rooted separation anxiety in an adult. *Journal of Behavior Therapy and Experimental Psychiatry, 14*, 61–65.

Clayton, P. J. (1990). Bereavement and depression. *Journal of Clinical Psychiatry, 51*, 34–38.

Diagnostic and Statistical Manual of Mental Disorders (4th ed.). (1994). Washington, DC: American Psychiatric Press, Inc.

Figley, C. R., Bride, B. E., & Mazza, N. (Eds.). (1997). Death and trauma: The traumatology of grieving. Washington, DC. Taylor and Francis.

Freud, S. (1953). Mourning and melancholia. In J. Strachey (Ed. and Trans.), *The standard edition, volume 14.* (pp. 243–258). London: Hogarth.

Guze, S. B. (1970). The role of follow up studies: Their contribution to diagnostic classification as applied to hysteria. *Seminars in Psychiatry, 2*, 392–402.

Horowitz, M. J. (1976). *Stress response syndromes.* New York: Jason Aronson Inc.

Horowitz, M. J., Wilner, N., & Alvarez, W. (1979). Impact of event scale: A measure of subjective stress. *Psychosomatic Medicine, 41*, 209–218.

Horowitz, M. J., Marmar, C., Weiss, D. S. (1984). Brief psychotherapy of bereavement reactions: The relationship of process to outcome. *Archives of General Psychiatry, 41*, 438–448.

Horowitz, M., Bonanno, G., & Holen, A. (1993). Pathological grief: Diagnosis and explanation. *Psychosomatic Medicine, 55*, 260–273.

Horowitz, M. J., Siegel, B., Holen, A., Bonnano, G. A., Milbrath, C., & Stinson, C. H. (1997). Diagnostic criteria for complicated grief disorder. *American Journal of Psychiatry, 154*, 904–910.

Kim, K., & Jacobs, S. C. (1991). Pathologic grief and its relationship to other psychiatric disorders. *Journal of Affective Disorders, 21*, 257–263.

Lindeman, E. (1944). Symptomatology and management of acute grief. *American Journal of Psychiatry, 101*, 141–148.

Manicavasagar, V., & Silove, D. (1997). Is there an adult form of separation anxiety disorder? A brief clinical report. *Australian and New Zealand Journal of Psychiatry, 31*, 299–303.

Middleton, W., Raphael, B., Martinek, N., & Misso, V. (1993). Pathological grief reactions. In: M. S. Stroebe, W. Stroebe, & R. O. Hansson, (Eds.), *Handbook of bereavement: Theory, research, and intervention.* New York: Cambridge University Press.

Middleton, W., Burnett, P., Raphael, B., & Martinek, N. (1996). The bereavement response—a cluster analysis. *British Journal of Psychiatry, 169*, 167–171.

Nader, K. O. (1997). Childhood traumatic loss: The interaction of trauma and grief. In C. R. Figley, B. E. Bride, N. Mazza (Eds.), *Death and trauma: The traumatology of grieving.* (pp. 17–41). Washington, DC: Taylor and Francis.

Ollendick, T. H., Lease, C. A., & Cooper, C. (1993). Separation anxiety in young adults: A preliminary examination. *Journal of Anxiety Disorders, 7*, 293–305.

Parkes, C. M. (1965). Bereavement and mental illness, part 2: A classification of bereavement reactions. *British Journal of Medical Psychology, 38,* 13–26.

Parkes, C. M. (1970). The first year of bereavement. A longitudinal study of the reaction of London widows to the death of their husbands. *Psychiatry, 33,* 444–467.

Parkes, C. M. (1972). *Bereavement: Studies of grief in adult life.* New York: International Universities Press.

Parkes, C. M., & Weiss, R. S. (1983). *Recovery from bereavement.* New York: Basic Books.

Prigerson, H. G., Maciejewski, P. K., Newsom, J., Reynolds, C. F., Frank, E., Bierhals, A. J., Miller, M. D., Fasiczka, A., Doman, J., & Houck, P. R. (1995a). The inventory of complicated grief: A scale to measure maladaptive symptoms of loss. *Psychiatry Research, 59,* 65–79.

Prigerson, H. G., Frank, E., Kasl, S. V., Reynolds, C. F., Anderson, B., Zubenko, G. S., Houck, P. R., George, C. J., & Kupfer, D. J. (1995b). Complicated grief and bereavement-related depression as distinct disorders: Preliminary empirical validation in elderly bereaved spouses. *American Journal of Psychiatry, 152,* 22–30.

Prigerson, H. G., Bierhals, A. J., Kasl, S. V., Reynolds, C. F., Shear, M. K., Newsom, J. T., & Jacobs, S. C. (1996). Complicated grief as a distinct disorder from bereavement-related depression and anxiety: A replication study. *The American Journal of Psychiatry, 153,* 1484–1486.

Prigerson, H. G., Bierhals, A. J., Kasl, S. V., Reynolds, C. F., Shear, M. K., Day, N., Beery, L. C., Newsom, J. T., & Jacobs, S. (1997). Traumatic grief as a risk factor for mental and physical morbidity. *American Journal of Psychiatry, 154,* 617–623.

Prigerson, H. G., Beery, L. C., Bridge, J., Rosenheck, R. A., Maciejewski, P. K., Kupfer, D. J., & Brent, D. (in press). Traumatic Grief as a risk factor for suicidal ideation among young adults. *American Journal of Psychiatry.*

Prigerson, H. G., Shear, M. K., Jacobs, S. C., Reynolds, C. F., Maciejewski, P. K., Pilkonis, P., Wortman, C., Williams, J. B. W., Widiger, T. A., Davidson, J., Frank, E., Kupfer, D. J., Zisook, S. (in press). Consensus criteria for Traumatic Grief: A preliminary empirical test. *British Journal of Psychiatry.*

Prigerson, H. G., & Jacobs, S. C. (in press). Diagnostic criteria for Traumatic Grief: Conceptual issues, critical appraisal, and an empirical test. In M. S. Stroebe, W. Stroebe, R. O. Hansson, & H. Schut (Eds.), *New handbook of bereavement: Consequences, coping and care.* Washington, DC: American Psychological Association Press.

Pynoos, R. S., & Nader, K. (1990). Children's exposure to violence and traumatic death. *Psychiatric Annals, 20,* 334–344.

Rando, T. A. (1993). *Treatment of complicated mourning.* Champaign, Ill: Research Press.

Raphael, B., & Middleton, W. (1990). What is pathologic grief? *Psychiatric Annals, 20,* 304–307.

Raphael, B., & Martinek, N. (1997). Assessing traumatic bereavement and post-traumatic stress disorder. In J. P. Wilson, T. M. Keane (Eds.), *Assessing Psychological Trauma and PTSD.* New York: The Guilford Press.

Silove, D., Manicavasagar, V., O'Connell, D., Blaszczynski, A., Wagner, R., & Henry, J. (1993). The development of the separation anxiety symptom inventory (SASI). *Australian and New Zealand Journal of Psychiatry, 27,* 477–488.

Wortman, C. B., & Silver, R. C. (1989). The myths of coping with loss. *Journal of Consulting and Clinical Psychology, 57,* 349–357.

Zisook, S., & Lyons, L. (1989). Bereavement and unresolved grief in psychiatric outpatients. *Omega, 20,* 307–322.

Diagnosis of Traumatic Grief

The four main diagnostic criteria for Traumatic Grief are listed in Table 1. Criterion A specifies that the symptoms of the disorder occur in the circumstances of the death of a significant other. It also requires that intrusive, distressing separation anxiety is present. Criterion B includes 11 symptoms that are bereavement specific manifestations of having been traumatized by the death. Criterion C specifies that the duration of the symptomatic disturbance must be at least 2 months. Criterion D requires that the symptomatic disturbance cause clinically significant impairment in social, occupational, or other important areas of functioning. The criteria are designed to distinguish Traumatic Grief from other disorders and from normal grief, in a conservative approach to diagnosis.

This chapter provides a review of each criterion, including each item under the 4 main criteria, as well as a discussion of how the criteria presented are linked together in making a diagnosis of Traumatic Grief during assessment. In addition, this chapter presents differential diagnosis, associated descriptive features of Traumatic Grief, associated physical and general medical conditions, associated laboratory findings, the course of the disorder, and the prognosis of the disorder.

☐ Death of a Significant Other and Symptoms of Separation Anxiety: Criterion A

Criterion A contains two parts that are essential for the diagnosis of Traumatic Grief. The first part, A1, addresses the death of a significant other

---

TABLE 1   Proposed Criteria for Traumatic Grief

Criterion A:
1. Person has experienced the death of a significant other.
2. The response involves intrusive, distressing preoccupation with the deceased person (e.g., yearning, longing, or searching).

Criterion B:
In response to the death, the following symptoms are marked and persistent:
1. Frequent efforts to avoid reminders of the deceased (e.g., thoughts, feelings, activities, people, places).
2. Purposelessness or feelings of futility about the future.
3. Subjective sense of numbness, detachment, or absence of emotional responsiveness.
4. Feeling stunned, dazed, or shocked.
5. Difficulty acknowledging the death (e.g., disbelief).
6. Feeling that life is empty or meaningless.
7. Difficulty imagining a fulfilling life without the deceased.
8. Feeling that part of oneself has died.
9. Shattered world view (e.g., lost sense of security, trust, or control).
10. Assumes symptoms or harmful behaviors of, or related to, the deceased person.
11. Excessive irritability, bitterness, or anger related to the death.

Criterion C:
The duration of disturbance (symptoms listed) is at least two months.

Criterion D:
The disturbance causes clinically significant impairment in social, occupational, or other important areas of functioning.

---

as the essential context for the diagnosis, and the other part, A2, specifies symptoms of separation anxiety that are essential for diagnosis.

A1 requires that a person experience the death of a significant other in order to qualify for diagnosis. Losses other than a death, such as loss of a home, loss of a job, divorce, loss of a limb, or loss of health, do not qualify for the diagnosis. The symptoms of Traumatic Grief may be caused by a sudden, unexpected, or violent death. However, the death need not have been objectively traumatic in order to make the diagnosis (Horowitz, Marmar, Weiss, DeWitt, & Rosenbaum, 1984; Horowitz et al., 1997). Symptoms of Traumatic Grief might follow any death that is personally devastating. In this case, the devastation caused by the death is related more to the relationship to the deceased and other personal vulnerability factors in contrast to the instance of an obviously violent death. In most cases, an amalgamation of both environmental and personal elements contributes to the occurrence of a disorder. In short, whether the origin of Traumatic Grief is mainly in the nature of the death or personal vulnerability, the nucleus of the disorder is a traumatic separation.

The term "significant other" refers to anyone the bereaved person identifies as a person with whom they had a close and confiding relationship. This might include immediate family, first degree relatives, and intimate friends and supports. This definition relies on the subjective judgment of the bereaved person. No better foundation suggests itself. Attempts to list objectively all the variations of "significant other" become laborious and pedantic. This criterion is designed to include a range of relationships that become significant for adults, not only those to family and first degree relatives, but also other intimates.

A2 requires intrusive and distressing core symptoms of separation anxiety for making the diagnosis of Traumatic Grief. Note that the ensuing discussion builds on the section in chapter 1 that introduced the concept of separation anxiety as part of a broader review of attachment behavior. A2 requires that the bereaved person with Traumatic Grief have symptoms of intrusive, distressing preoccupations with the deceased person. The symptoms manifest themselves in episodic pangs of yearning, longing, or pining for the person who is lost. Searching is the behavioral counterpart of preoccupation and yearning and has been related to hypervigilant, environmental scanning for cues of the deceased person. Searching involves a feeling of being drawn to and seeking out places and things identified with the deceased person as if for the sake of regaining what has been lost. In the circumstances of a death, searching behavior, which is often nonverbal and unconscious, inevitably ends in frustration, usually triggering another pang of grief. Separation anxiety is different from generalized anxiety and panic by virtue of being focused on a death and being context specific.

The symptoms in A2 are the most frequent and pervasive symptoms of Traumatic Grief without which the diagnosis cannot be made. In this sense, they are essential. It can be argued that they are the unique and essential elements of normal grief itself, without which normal grief does not occur. In the case of Traumatic Grief, in contrast to normal grief, the separation anxiety persists at a marked level of intensity, remains intrusive and distressing, and, along with other symptoms, interferes with social, occupational, and other important areas of functioning.

☐ Bereavement Specific Symptoms of Traumatization by a Death: Criterion B

Criterion B specifies 11 symptoms that reflect the bereavement specific, personal devastation caused by the death of a significant other. It describes a domain of traumatic distress that is distinct from separation distress and that is required for diagnosis (Raphael & Martinek, 1997). All of the symptoms when present as part of Criterion B must be marked and persistent to justify inclusion under this symptomatic criterion.

The symptoms of traumatic distress under criterion B relate to feelings of being devastated by the death. The group of symptoms under Criterion B can be a function of the high intensity and insecurity of the preexisting attachment to the deceased person and the previous reliance on the bereaved person on the deceased person for providing meaning to life, as well as fulfilling a variety of practical purposes. Or, they can be a function of objective, traumatic qualities of the death that shake the working assumptions that a person makes in daily life and about ongoing attachments. Or, finally, the symptoms can be a function of both, which is often the case.

Of the 11 symptoms under Criterion B, 4 reflect marked and persistent avoidance of the death and emotional numbing. B1 is frequent efforts to avoid reminders of the deceased. B3 is a subjective sense of numbness, detachment, or absence of emotional responsiveness, and B4 is feeling stunned, dazed, or shocked. B5 is defined as difficulty acknowledging the death (e.g., disbelief), reflects the cognitive dissonance caused by the death, and is related to these items.

Several of the items reflect the marked and persistent disorganization of subjective experience and behavior patterns that occur in Traumatic Grief. B2 is purposelessness or feelings of futility about the future. Most bereaved persons whose behavior and social activities had been tied closely to the deceased person have some sense of the uselessness of behavior patterns previously linked to the deceased person. These feelings are ordinarily transient during acute bereavement, and B2 is designed to reflect marked, persistent levels of this feeling. B6 is feeling that life is empty or meaningless. B7 is difficulty imagining a fulfilling life without the deceased. Both of these items extend from B2 and reflect the degree to which the bereaved person's assumptive world is shaken by the death. B8 is feeling that part of oneself has died, reflecting identification with the deceased, identity confusion or depletion, and a sense of lifelessness or dismemberment caused by the death. B9 is a shattered world view (e.g., lost sense of security, trust, or control), resulting from the death.

B10 is the assumption of symptoms or harmful behaviors of, or related to, the deceased person. This symptom stems from well known observations of grief facsimile symptoms (or identification symptoms), in which bereaved persons take on symptomatic aspects of the terminal illness of the deceased person. When this symptom emerges, often after frightening or violent, gruesome, disfiguring modes of death, it is usually an indication of traumatic distress in reaction to the death of the deceased. This symptom per se is not commonly observed. When it does occur, it is highly specific for Traumatic Grief, serving to differentiate Traumatic Grief from normal grief. This item in the diagnostic criteria for Traumatic Grief is defined to be broader and includes a wider range of maladaptive behaviors related to the deceased person and applicable in the circumstances of sudden, unexpected deaths when no terminal illness has occurred. Thus, this item includes both facsimile illness symptoms and the assumption of harmful behaviors of, or related to, the deceased person.

B11 is excessive irritability, bitterness, or anger related to the death. This symptom is rooted in the insecurity created by a death. Bereaved persons report feelings about the unfairness of the death. They often complain to or challenge authority figures such as the physician or therapist. There may be a quality of protest in these complaints. Protest, as a close accompaniment of separation anxiety, is discussed more in chapter 1.

☐ Severity of Symptoms for Both Criteria A and B

The consensus criteria for Traumatic Grief used two strategies to address the severity of symptoms required for diagnosis. One strategy addresses the severity of each symptom and the other, the number of symptoms required for diagnosis. First, as already noted, to address the intensity of the symptoms, the criteria specify that symptoms must be "marked" and "persistent" in order to qualify as diagnostic elements. While this standard is somewhat vague, it is consistent with the strategy used in DSM-IV and conforms to ordinary clinical practice.

Second, to address the number of symptoms necessary for a diagnosis of Traumatic Grief, analyses of the consensus criteria in a sample of 306 San Diego widowed persons have established preliminary, working thresholds for both Criteria A2 and B (Prigerson, Maciejewski, Pilkonis, Wortman, Williams, Widiger, Davidson, Frank, Kupfer, Zisook, in press). The analyses were completed using an available data set that included all the symptoms (or proxies) except one of the items in Criterion B. Based on these analyses, 3 symptoms of the 4 under Criterion A2 (among preoccupation, yearning, longing, or searching) should be present for diagnosis.

For Criterion B, 4 of the 11 symptoms itemized under this criterion should be present (Prigerson et al., in press). Of note, several symptoms of Criterion B did not operate well in these analyses. These included "difficulty imagining a fulfilling life," "feeling that part of oneself has died," and the avoidance item. If these preliminary analyses are confirmed, it suggests that the total number of items listed under Criterion

B would be reduced in the future. Specifically, the avoidance item might be eliminated, and the other items just noted might be consolidated with "purposelessness or feelings of futility" into one item. This would leave a total of 8 diagnostic items under Criterion B, and the future standard might be 4 of these 8 symptoms for diagnosis. Future field trials will need to test competing algorithms extensively. For the time being, it seems most sensible to leave all the items determined by the consensus conference under Criterion B, recommend a threshold of 4 symptoms, and wait for more data.

☐ Issue of Duration: Criterion C

The diagnostic criteria for Traumatic Grief specify a duration of at least 2 months for the syndromal, symptomatic disturbance in order to make a diagnosis. Criterion C is an important supplement to the severity of symptoms for setting off Traumatic Grief from normal grief. The 2 month criterion is consistent with a recent analysis and conclusions of a longitudinal study in Australia that documents a major decline on average in separation anxiety in 1 to 3 months (Middleton, 1995; Raphael & Martinek, 1997).

It is important to note that this criterion is not anchored to the date of death although Criterion A1 does require that the person has experienced the death of a significant other. It is conceivable, therefore, that symptoms of Traumatic Grief may have their onset before a death occurs. However, the diagnosis cannot be made solely on the basis of anticipatory symptoms.

Two major concerns entered into the thinking of the consensus panel when they considered this criterion. Clinicians who evaluate these patients will face the same dilemma. One concern was not to encroach into the range of normal grief. Counterbalancing this was a conviction that initial reactions to a death often prove to be the best predictors of diagnosis and prognosis. In brief, the expert panel believed that it would be inhumane to let bereaved persons with Traumatic Grief suffer longer than necessary.

More studies of the natural history of normal and Traumatic Grief which will lead to knowledge of factors that determine failure to spontaneously resolve normal grief will be useful for determining who warrants diagnosis and treatment, and when. This will lead to refinement of Criterion C for the duration of symptomatic disturbance. The clinical literature on pathologic grief suggests several potential factors that determine a long course of illness. These include fear of losing control (Clayton, Halikas, &

Maurice, 1971), facsimile symptoms (Zisook & DeVaul, 1977), personality traits, such as insecure attachment style (Bowlby, 1969) particularly in interaction with the loss of a security enhancing attachment figure (Horowitz, Widner, & Marmar, 1980), neuroticism (Raphael & Middleton, 1990; Stroebe & Strobe, 1987; Vachon et al., 1982), and low sense of internal control (Stroebe and Stroebe, 1987). While awaiting more data on risk factors established specifically for Traumatic Grief, the clinician making a diagnosis can judiciously use the ones I have just suggested to support the 2 month criterion for duration of the syndrome.

☐ Impairment in Psychosocial Functioning: Criterion D

With Criterion D, the diagnostic criteria for Traumatic Grief require that the symptomatic disturbance itemized in Criteria A2 and B cause clinically significant impairment in social, occupational, or other important areas of functioning. Criterion D, similar to Criterion C, is an important supplement to the severity of symptoms for differentiating Traumatic Grief from normal grief.

Most acutely bereaved persons experience transient disruption in psychosocial functioning. If this persists, it can become the main motivation for seeking an evaluation, sometimes at the initiative of the patient and other times under pressure to seek help from family, friends, or co-workers.

☐ Variations in the Pattern of Traumatic Grief

The literature on pathologic grief suggests there are severe, chronic, and delayed variations in the pattern of the disorder (Wortman & Silver, 1989; Raphael and Middleton, 1990; Middleton, Raphael, Martinek, & Misso, 1993; Middleton, Burnett, Raphael, & Martinek, 1996; Parkes, 1970; Parkes & Weiss, 1983; Byrne & Raphael, 1994). To cover these possible variations in the pattern of Traumatic Grief, the consensus criteria are designed to diagnose severe and chronic patterns of the disorder. For the purpose of diagnosis, the consensus criteria do not specifically provide for a delayed variation in the pattern of Traumatic Grief. Nevertheless, a clinician evaluating a patient sometime during the first 6 months of bereavement who suspects there is a risk for clinical complications or is left with doubt about the diagnosis, should monitor the course of grief periodically during this 6 months in order to pick up a delayed onset disorder if one occurs.

☐ Anniversaries of the Death

If the diagnosis of Traumatic Grief is missed during the first year of bereavement, the first anniversary and subsequent anniversaries of the death are landmarks which often help in making the diagnosis later in the course of illness. Typically, there is an exacerbation of symptoms lasting a few days around anniversaries (Jacobs et al., 1987) and, sometimes, key holidays. Indeed, there may be a transient impairment in psychosocial functioning as well. While most bereaved persons will find anniversaries of a death a difficult period, it is those for whom the anniversary looms as an overwhelming nemesis or for whom the anniversary distress is severe, prolonged, and persistently disruptive of psychosocial functioning, that a careful evaluation will lead to the diagnosis of Traumatic Grief (Jacobs et al., 1987).

☐ Associated Descriptive Features

The existing literature on pathologic grief provides a foundation for beginning to understand and study the associated descriptive features of Traumatic Grief. Still, this literature is usually based on symptom scores, unstructured diagnostic assessments, or working diagnostic criteria sets developed specifically for a particular study. Therefore, the observations described next require verification in studies using the new diagnostic criteria for Traumatic Grief.

Having stated this caveat, there is strong suggestive evidence that multiple symptoms might be associated with Traumatic Grief. These include guilt over omissions during the terminal illness (Parkes, 1970), survivor guilt (Prigerson et al., 1995a), despair (Prigerson et al., 1995a), suicidal ideation and self-destructive behavior, the loss of previously sustained beliefs (Wortman and Silver, 1989), non-specific somatic symptoms (Lindeman, 1944; Parkes, 1970), anger and protest at authority figures (Lindeman, 1944; Bowlby, 1963; Prigerson, Bierhals, Wolfson, Ehrenpreis, & Reynolds, 1997a), wooden and formal efforts to control emotion (Lindeman, 1944), neurovegetative symptoms (Lindeman, 1944), over-activity without a sense of loss (Lindeman, 1944), anxiety (Anderson, 1949; Zisook, Schneider, & Schuchter, 1990), and feelings of insecurity (Bowlby, 1969). There may be a transient loss of interest in relationships to others

(Lindeman, 1944) and social withdrawal (Lindeman, 1944; Prigerson et al., 1995a). other aspects of maladaptive relationships to others may be anxious attachment (Bowlby, 1969), compulsive care giving (Bowlby, 1969), or counterphobic risk taking as survivors attempt to overcome their fear of the deceased person's death (Lindeman, 1944; Parkes & Weiss, 1983).

☐ Associated Physical Findings and General Medical Conditions

The facial expression of grief is characterized by raising of the inner aspects of the eyebrows, horizontal wrinkling of the forehead, wrinkling at the base of the nose, and depression of the angles of the mouth (Darwin, 1872). This expression of separation anxiety may be a compromise between an urge to cry and an attempt to suppress it. It appears to be unique to the circumstances of a death or loss. The facies of separation anxiety is distinct from a worried or a depressed facies. In addition, this facial expression is distinct from a post traumatic disorder facies (Raphael & Martinek, 1997). The absence of this facial expression does not negate the diagnosis of Traumatic Grief as some persons may have a flat, expressionless visage, or a superimposed depressive or worried facies from a comorbid disorder.

Whether the subset of bereaved persons with Traumatic Grief carry a high risk of morbidity and mortality is little studied. The epidemiologic literature on bereavement, which does not differentiate between normal and Traumatic Grief, indicates a high risk of mortality from multiple causes. The risk of mortality occurs largely within the first two years after a death (Jacobs & Ostfeld, 1977; Stroebe & Strobe, 1993). One exception is suicide for which the mortality risk is prolonged for years among bereaved persons (MacMahon and Pugh, 1965; Conwell, Rotenburg, & Caine, 1990; Kaprio, Koskenvuo, & Rita, 1987).

In a recent study of bereaved spouses, those with Traumatic Grief are a subgroup at significantly elevated risk of morbidity (Prigerson et al., 1997b). This study indicates that Traumatic Grief predicts a higher risk of suicidal ideation, heart trouble, high systolic blood pressure, cancer, and high risk health behaviors such as excess consumption of food, alcohol, and tobacco. In a companion study, widowers by comparison with widows have a higher risk of accidents, heart disease, and cancer, although widows had higher mean levels of psychiatric symptoms (Chen, Bierhals, Prigerson, Kasl, Masare, Jacobs, Psychological Medicine, in press). Finally, high Traumatic Grief scores predict physical functional impairment (Prigerson et al., 1995a). These results were found in a sample including some who had no increased morbidity, suggesting it is not the state of bereavement but rather the Traumatic Grief in reaction to the death that is an essential, intermediate step that puts individuals at risk for physical and functional impairment in the postdeath period.

☐ Associated Laboratory Findings

Persistently high levels of separation distress are associated with high urinary, free cortisol-excretion (Jacobs et al., 1984). One study of acute bereavement observed nonsuppression on the dexamethasone suppression test (DST), which was associated with high anxiety scores, not depressive symptoms (Shuchter, Zisook, Kirkorowicz, & Risch, 1986). Traumatic Grief is associated with self-reported symptoms of sleep impairment (McDermott, Prigerson, & Reynolds, 1997; Prigerson et al., 1997b). The intrusive thoughts of Traumatic Grief and avoidance of reminders are significantly associated with prolonged sleep latency and impaired delta sleep ratio, but not with depression scores (McDermott et al., 1997; Hall et al., 1997).

☐ Course and Prognosis

Without skilled professional intervention, the course of Traumatic Grief is chronic and unremitting (Prigerson et al., 1995a and b). Severe disturbance usually begins at the time of a death and does not decline significantly thereafter (Wortman & Silver, 1989; Prigerson et al., 1997b). Preliminary evidence suggests that a disturbance may emerge before the actual death (Prigerson et al., 1997b). For some, after a mild or moderately intense onset, the intensity of Traumatic Grief peaks 6 months after a death and remains high 25 months into bereavement and possibly beyond (Prigerson et al., 1997b). Those for whom the disorder has not resolved significantly following the first anniversary of the death will have a prolonged course for 2 years and probably beyond (Prigerson et al., 1997b).

As bereaved persons are reluctant to seek help and in the absence of systematic screening, diagnosis is often made late in the course of Traumatic Grief when a chronic disorder of 2–3 years duration exists.

☐ Differential Diagnosis of Traumatic Grief

This presentation of differential diagnosis of Traumatic Grief is a logical discussion based on the defined, qualitative differences among the clinical syndromes that can occur during acute bereavement. Empirical studies supporting the differentiation of Traumatic Grief from other disorders are reviewed in the previous and the next chapters (chapters 2 and 4). While the following discussion of differential diagnosis can serve as a starting point for clinical practice, it will be important to empirically test these guidelines over the next few years using consensus diagnostic criteria in bereaved patient populations that have clinical complications.

Circumstances of the Disorder

Traumatic Grief occurs in the circumstances of the death of a significant other. If the syndrome of Traumatic Grief occurs exclusively during the course of another disorder, such as a psychotic disorder or severe depression, the diagnosis of Traumatic Grief would not be given unless an intercurrent, significant death occurred.

Other disorders can occur in the circumstances of a death including Major Depressive Episodes, Panic Disorders, Generalized Anxiety Disorders, and Post-traumatic Stress Disorders (particularly when the death is associated with violence). When these disorders are present, a cooccurring diagnosis can be made. In addition to the discussion below, these potentially comorbid disorders are reviewed in more detail in the next chapter.

Major Depressive Disorder

While neurovegetative symptoms can occur in both Traumatic Grief and Major Depression, a Major Depressive Episode is distinguished from Traumatic Grief by the pervasive, depressed mood disturbance (in contrast to the episodic pangs of grief), depressive cognitive schemata, and a disturbance of self-esteem reflected in feelings of worthlessness and pervasive feelings of guilt. The characteristic features of Traumatic Grief are not present.

Panic Disorder

Panic Disorder is distinguished from Traumatic Grief by severe episodes of anxiety (panic attacks) that occur frequently in public places, often in association with agoraphobia. Separation distress is not present. Also, the traumatic symptoms of Traumatic Grief under Criterion B are absent in Panic Disorder.

Generalized Anxiety Disorder

Generalized Anxiety Disorder is distinguished from Traumatic Grief by its occurrence in circumstances other than a death. Specific cognition focused on the death, separation distress, and the traumatic symptoms of Traumatic Grief are absent.

Post-traumatic Stress Disorder

Several aspects of Traumatic Grief distinguish it from a post traumatic stress syndrome. In Traumatic Grief, the core symptoms include separation anxiety. The symptoms of separation anxiety might be construed as reexperiencing, which is 1 of the 3 domains of Post-traumatic Stress Disorder (PTSD). However, in the case of Traumatic Grief, the symptoms of separation anxiety are a function of a wish to be reunited with the deceased person, i.e., pining and searching for the lost person, rather than an intrusive, fearful reexperiencing of a horrifying event (Raphael & Martinek, 1977). Furthermore, in Traumatic Grief, symptoms of avoidance, a second domain of PTSD symptoms, are not prominent. Indeed, in preliminary analyses of the items under Criterion B, the symptom of avoidance had low specificity, low item-whole correlations, and a diminished Chronbach's alpha with its inclusion in the criteria set (Prigerson, Maciejewski, Pilkonis, Wortman, Williams, Widiger, Davidson, Frank, Kupfer, Zisook, in press). For the time being, while awaiting field trials of alternate diagnostic algorithms, the consensus panel agreed that the symptom of avoidance should be included among the other symptoms of Criterion B without giving it prominence. In further contrast to PTSD, there is no evidence of hyperaroused sleep patterns among persons with intense symptoms of Traumatic Grief (McDermott et al., 1997). Also, hypervigilance as part of Traumatic Grief relates to scanning the environment for cues of the deceased person rather than monitoring potential threats of a recurrent horrifying event. Finally, as noted in chapters 2 and 3 in the discussion of two pathways to the disorder, the diagnosis of Traumatic Grief does not require the death of a significant other to have been violent and horrific. Thus, the syndrome of Traumatic Grief, while having a passing resemblance to PTSD, occurring sometimes after a violent death, and coexisting sometimes with PTSD, is distinct.

In the event of a violent death, or simply a sudden, unexpected death, a full spectrum of PTSD symptoms might emerge, including symptoms from all three domains of reexperiencing, hyperarousal, and avoidance. PTSD is distinguished from Traumatic Grief by its occurrence in other traumatic contexts than a death. Also, PTSD criteria do not include symptoms of separation anxiety. In addition, there is a distinct quality of the symptoms of traumatization in PTSD, in contrast to Traumatic Grief. In PTSD, the symptoms relate to a horrific, violent, life threatening event. In Traumatic Grief, the symptoms, listed under Criterion B, are related to a traumatic separation and feelings of having been devastated by the death. Finally, as noted above, symptoms of avoidance and hyperarousal are more conspicuous in PTSD.

Psychotic Illness

While the perceptual disturbances of Traumatic Grief (illusions, hallucinations) can be misconstrued as symptoms of psychosis, the perceptual disturbance is focused on the deceased person and a thought disorder and delusions are absent. For example, the perceptual disturbances are often based on an actual stimulus such as the illusion of encountering the deceased person in a group on a crowded street. They often occur in special places associated with the deceased person, and are reversed by the intrusion of reality or the availability of substitute attachment figures.

Normal Grief

Probably the strongest strategy for avoiding false positive diagnosis involves the judgment that must be made to recognize normal grief and differentiate it from Traumatic Grief. In normal grief, a progression of the multiple dimensions of grief occurs (see chapter 1) with a reduction in the dysphoria of separation distress and traumatic distress, growing acceptance of the death, and the gradual return of the capacity for reinvestment in new interests, activities, and relationships.

In contrast, Traumatic Grief is characterized under Criterion A by intrusive and distressing separation anxiety. Also, Traumatic Grief is qualitatively and quantitatively differentiated from normal grief by virtue of symptoms related to feelings of devastation caused by the death and itemized under Criterion B. Finally, all symptoms of Traumatic Grief under Criteria A and B are linked to Criteria C on prolonged duration and Criterion D on impairment in social and occupational functioning. Criteria C and D distinguish Traumatic Grief from normal grief by requiring substantial prolongation of symptoms and impairment in functioning.

When using the consensus diagnostic criteria, coping phenomena are secondary for the purpose of diagnosis. A bereaved person copes with a death with both conscious and unconscious strategies (Jacobs, 1993, Jacobs, Kasl, Schaefer, & Ostfeld, 1994). Conscious cognitive and behavioral coping can be active or passive and problem focused or emotion focused. Unconscious ego defensive coping can be mature or neurotic and effective or not in modulating emotion. Both types of coping can be adaptive or maladaptive. The relationship of coping to poor outcome is complex and suggests that different types of coping are necessary for different phases of bereavement and for different specific outcomes (Jacobs, 1993; Jacobs et al., 1994). Sensitivity to the coping strategies of a patient is useful for ensuring adherence to treatment and for some psychotherapeutic purposes, but is not essential for the descriptive diagnosis embodied in the consensus criteria. It is useful to pay attention to coping in treatment, and it is discussed more in chapter 6 as part of a diagnosis treatment algorithm.

Clinical Example

Mrs. B.: a bereaved person meeting criteria for Traumatic Grief, but not for Major Depressive Disorder, Post-traumatic Stress Disorder, or Panic Disorder.

Mrs. B. was a 59-year-old businesswoman whose husband died suddenly and unexpectedly from a cardiac arrhythmia secondary to a pulmonary embolus. She presented for evaluation two and a half months after the death of her husband, when her separation distress was intensifying. She had some depressive symptoms, including depressed mood, mild appetite disturbance, and difficulty falling asleep, but did not meet criteria for a major depressive episode. She had a few nighttime panic attacks 3 months after the death which were associated with the fear that she would lose her mind. These subsided over a month.

She had some traumatic symptoms, which did not meet criteria for Post-traumatic Stress Disorder. These included intrusive images of the circumstances of her husband's death, described here. While at home and with no forewarning, she heard a thud in an adjoining room in her home, realized something was dreadfully wrong, found her husband unconscious, and "knew immediately that he was dead." She described the feelings associated with this as a "stabbing injury" and a "shock" and differentiated it from the separation distress described below. This was the emotional material she avoided most strenuously during evaluation and in therapy. In addition, she described how she now circumscribed her life to avoid persons and places that reminded her of her loss. She reported a sleep disturbance and apprehension about additional unexpected events. She described herself variously as being in a state of "alarm" or "panic."

She could not accept the death. She described the cognitive dissonance of realizing that her husband was dead and yet not being able to believe it, a state of mind that prevailed for months. She identified her deceased husband as a source of security for her, an idea that was rooted in part by his profession and membership in a protective community. His death left her feeling alone, deeply insecure, and unsafe. She was unsure about her ability and desire to carry on her responsibilities as a widowed mother and grandmother in her extended family of adult children. These roles no longer had the same meaning as when her husband was alive. She felt "angry and cheated" out of a happy, meaningful, and secure retirement by the death of her husband. In these feelings, there was a quality of protest over her sad fate.

She sought treatment because of symptoms of intensifying separation distress. These included intense yearning and crying for her deceased husband which made her feel "like crawling out of her skin" and made her wonder "how much can I take." The feelings were unbidden, swelled in intensity for five minutes or so, and subsided over a half hour. The feelings arose typically at home at times when she would have expected her husband to arrive, or in the little daily rituals such as setting the table for dinner that were strongly associated with him. She felt compelled to spend her evenings at home where she felt closest to her deceased husband and where she nurtured the vague hope that he might return. This realization crystallized in therapy as she constructed her motivation for the behavior of staying at home so much and tried to explain to herself why she had little interest in social activities and chose not to go out with friends. On other occasions, she would visit his place of work as if she might find him there. As all her symptoms intensified, she wondered if she would be able to keep going and get herself to work each morning. The symptoms did not begin immediately and intensely after the death when the family rallied around and she needed to "get through the holidays." They were active for a month when she presented for evaluation and continued unabated for 2 months and beyond, during initial monitoring and then therapy. The first and second anniversaries of her husband's death were marked by an exacerbation of symptoms and return to treatment.

This widowed woman did not meet criteria for the diagnosis of a Major Depressive Episode, nor for Panic Disorder, nor for Post-traumatic Stress Disorder at the time of initial evaluation. She clearly met the criteria for the diagnosis of Traumatic Grief by meeting 3 of the criteria under Criterion A, 7 of the criteria under Criterion B, and both Criteria C and D.

Conclusion

As noted in chapter 2 and to some extent in the above discussion, the consensus diagnostic criteria for Traumatic Grief discussed in this chapter need additional study and refinement to resolve important questions that the consensus panel was not able to answer with data. In the meantime, the criteria set described above can begin not only to serve the needs of clinicians confronted with bereaved patients seeking evaluation and treatment but also researchers who will provide answers to the remaining, unanswered questions about diagnosis of this disorder. These working criteria provide a basis for beginning to think diagnostically about Traumatic Grief. Diagnostic thinking is important because of its implications for psychopharmacologic and psychotherapeutic treatments. The next 3 chapters provide additional perspectives on how to use the diagnostic criteria for Traumatic Grief.

☐ References

Anderson, C. (1949). Aspects of pathological grief and mourning. *International Journal of Psychoanalysis, 30,* 48–55.

Bowlby, J. (1963). Pathological mourning and childhood mourning. *Journal of the American Psychoanalytic Association, 11,* 500–541.

Bowlby, J. (1969). *Attachment and loss, vol 1: Attachment.* New York: Basic Books.

Byrne, G., & Raphael, B. (1994). A longitudinal study of bereavement phenomena in recently widowed elderly men. *Psychological Medicine, 24,* 411–421.

Chen, J. H., Bierhals, A. J., Prigerson, H. G., Kasl, S. V., Masare, C. M., Jacobs, S. C.: Gender difference in the effects of bereavement-related psychological distress on health outcomes. *Psychological Medicine,* in press.

Clayton, P. J., Halikas, J. A., & Maurice, W. L. (1971). The bereavement of the widowed. *Diseases of the Nervous System, 32,* 597–604.

Conwell, Y., Rotenburg, M., & Caine, E. D. (1990). Completed suicide at age 50 and over. *Journal of the American Geriatrics Society, 38,* 640–644.

Darwin, C. (1872). *The expression of the emotions in man and animals.* London: John Murray.

Hall, M., Reynolds, C. F., Buysse, D. J., Prigerson, H. G., Dew, M. A., & Kupfer, D. J. (1997). Intrusive thoughts and avoidance behaviors predict sleep disturbances in bereavement-related depression. *Depression and Anxiety, 6,* 106–112.

Horowitz, M. J., Wilner, N., & Marmar, C. (1980). Pathological grief and the activation of latent self-images. *American Journal of Psychiatry, 137,* 1157–1162.

Horowitz, M. J., Marmar, C., Weiss, D. S., DeWitt, K. N., & Rosenbaum, R. (1984). Brief psychotherapy of bereavement reactions: The relationship of process to outcome. *Archives of General Psychiatry, 41,* 438–448.

Horowitz, M. J., Siegel, B., Holen, A., Bonnano, G. A., Milbrath, C., & Stinson, C. H. (1997). Diagnostic criteria for complicated grief disorder. *American Journal of Psychiatry, 154,* 904–910.

Jacobs, S., & Ostfeld, A. (1977). An epidemiological review of the mortality of bereavement. *Psychosomatic Medicine, S39,* 344–357.

Jacobs, S. C., Mason, J., Kosten, T., Brown, S., Ostfeld, A. M. (1984). Urinary free cortical excretion in relation to age in acutely stressed persons with depressive symptoms. *Psychosomatic Medicine, 46,* 213–221.

Jacobs, S. C., Schaefer, C. A., Ostfeld, A. M., Kasl, S., Berkman, L. (1987). The first anniversary of bereavement. *Israel Journal of Psychiatry and Related Sciences, 24,* 77–85.

Jacobs, S. C. (1993). *Pathologic grief: Maladaptation to loss.* Washington, DC: American Psychiatric Press.

Jacobs, S., Kasl, S., Schaefer, C., & Ostfeld, A. (1994). Conscious and unconscious coping with loss. *Psychosomatic Medicine, 56,* 557–563.

Kaprio, J., Koskenvuo, M., & Rita, H. (1987). Mortality after bereavement: A prospective study of 95,647 widowed persons. *American Journal of Public Health, 77,* 283–287.

Lindeman, E. (1944). Symptomatology and management of acute grief. *American Journal of Psychiatry, 101,* 141–148.

MacMahon, B., & Pugh, T. F. (1965). Suicide in the widowed. *American Journal of Epidemiology, 81,* 23–31.

McDermott, O., Prigerson, H. G., & Reynolds, C. F. (1997). EEG sleep in complicated grief and bereavement-related depression: A preliminary report. *Biological Psychiatry, 41,* 710–716.

Middleton, W., Raphael, B., Martinek, N., & Misso, V. (1993). Pathological grief reactions. In: M. S. Stroebe, W. Stroebe, & R. O. Hansson (Eds.), *Handbook of bereavement: Theory, research, and intervention* (pp. 44–61). New York: Cambridge University Press.

Middleton, W. (1995). Bereavement phenomenology and the processes of resolution. M. D. Thesis. University of Queensland, Bribane, Australia.

Middleton, W., Burnett, P., Raphael, B., & Martinek, N. (1996). The bereavement response—a cluster analysis. *British Journal of Psychiatry, 169,* 167–171.

Parkes, C. M. (1970). The first year of bereavement. A longitudinal study of the reaction of London widows to the death of their husbands. *Psychiatry, 33,* 444–446.

Parkes, C. M., & Weiss, R. S. (1983). *Recovery from bereavement.* New York: Basic Books.

Prigerson, H. G., Maciejewski, P. K., Newsom, J., Reynolds, C. F., Frank, E., Bierhals, A. J., Miller, M. D., Fasiczka, A., Doman, J., & Houck, P. R. (1995a). The inventory of complicated grief: A scale to measure maladaptive symptoms of loss. *Psychiatry Research, 59,* 65–79.

Prigerson, H. G., Frank, E., Kasl, S. V., Reynolds, C. F., Anderson, B., Zubenko, G. S., Houck, P. R., George, C. J., & Kupfer, D. J. (1995b). Complicated grief and bereavement-related depression as distinct disorders: Preliminary empirical validation in elderly bereaved spouses. *American Journal of Psychiatry, 152,* 22–30.

Prigerson, H. G., Bierhals, A. J., Wolfson, L., Ehrenpreis, L., & Reynolds, C. E. (1997a). Case histories of complicated grief. *Omega, 35,* 9–24.

Prigerson, H. G., Bierhals, A. J., Kasl, S. V., Reynolds, C. F., Shear, M. K., Day, N., Beery, L. C., Newsom, J. T., & Jacobs, S. (1997b). Traumatic grief as a risk factor for mental and physical morbidity. *American Journal of Psychiatry, 154,* 617–623.

Prigerson, H. G., Shear, M. K., Jacobs, S. C., Reynolds, C. F., Maciejewski, P. K., Pilkonis, P., Wortman, C., Williams, J. B. W., Widiger, T. A., Davidson, J., Frank, E., Kupfer, D. J., Zisook, S. (in press). Consensus criteria for traumatic grief: A preliminary empirical test. *British Journal of Psychiatry.*

Raphael, B., Middleton, W. (1990). What is pathologic grief? *Psychiatric Annals, 20,* 304–307.

Raphael, B., & Martinek, N. (1997). Assessing traumatic bereavement and post-traumatic stress disorder. In J. P. Wilson, & T. M. Keane (Eds.), *Assessing Psychological Trauma and PTSD.* (pp. 379–395). New York: Guilford Press.

Shuchter, S. R., Zisook, S., Kirkorowicz, C., & Risch, C. (1986). The dexamethasone suppression test in acute grief. *American Journal of Psychiatry, 143,* 879–881.

Stroebe, W., & Stroebe, M. S. (1987). *Bereavement and health.* New York: Cambridge University Press.

Stroebe, M. S., & Stroebe, W. (1993). The mortality of bereavement. In M. S. Stroebe, W. Stroebe, & R. O. Hansson (Eds.), *Handbook of bereavement: Theory, research, and intervention* (pp. 175–195). New York: Cambridge University Press.

Vachon, M. L. S., Sheldon, A. R., Lancee, W. J., Lyall, W. A. L., Sheldon, A. R., Freuman, S. J. J. (1982). Correlates of enduring distress patterns following bereavement: Social network, life situation and personality. *Psychological Medicine, 12,* 783–788.

Wortman, C. B., Silver, R. C. (1989). The myths of coping with loss. *Journal of Consulting and Clinical Psychology, 57,* 349–357.

Zisook, S., DeVaul, R. A. (1977). Grief related facsimile illness. *International Journal of Psychiatry Medicine, 7,* 329–336.

Zisook, S., Schneider, D., Schuchter, S. R. (1990). Anxiety and bereavement. *Psychiatric Medicine, 8,* 83–96.

Comorbidity: Psychiatric Disorders Associated with Traumatic Grief

This chapter provides a review of psychiatric disorders associated with Traumatic Grief. For the purposes of the chapter, associated psychiatric disorders are those disorders that can occur during acute bereavement and can be comorbid with Traumatic Grief. Often, patients presenting for evaluation and treatment will have more than one psychiatric diagnosis. While most clinicians probably would agree that comorbidity would complicate the treatment and outcome of Traumatic Grief, or, for that matter, any other disorder, the implications of having both Traumatic Grief and a coexisting psychiatric disorder needs further study to clarify the implications of comorbidity.This chapter discusses the implications of the diagnosis of comorbid disorders, as we now understand them, for evaluation and treatment. The focus of the discussion is mostly on Major Depression and Post-traumatic Stress Disorder; however, I also pay attention to anxiety disorders, alcohol abuse, suicidal ideation, and Schizophrenic Disorder.

☐ Associated Psychiatric Disorders

There is evidence that Major Depression, Panic Disorder, Generalized Anxiety Disorder, Post-traumatic Stress Disorder (PTSD), and possibly increased alcohol use and abuse not only occur during the period of acute bereavement, but also that the risk of their occurrence is higher during this period (Bornstein, Clayton, Halikas, Maurice, & Robins, 1973; Jacobs et al., 1989; Jacobs et al., 1990; Schut, de Keijser, van den Bout, Dijhuis, 1991; Zisook, Shuchter, Mulvilhill, 1990a; Zisook and Shuchter, 1991 and 1993; Byrne, 1995; Breslau et al., 1998). Given the higher risk of these disorders during bereavement, it is not surprising that comorbidity with Traumatic Grief exists.

The possible relationship between Traumatic Grief and other psychiatric disorders could be of two types. There could be simple coexistence of two disorders, in which each disorder might aggravate the other by prolonging or adding to the intensity of symptom distress. For example, many clinicians experienced in treating complications of bereavement note that a Major Depressive Episode or a PTSD syndrome can interfere with the evolution of normal grief, making it more distressful, and can aggravate the symptoms of Traumatic Grief (Rynearson, 1987; Rynearson, & McCreery, 1993; Rynearson, 1996; Raphael, Middleton, Martinek, & Misso, 1993; Pynoos & Nader, 1993; Rando, 1993).

Another possibility is a causative relationship in which one disaster predisposes to another. As before, in the absence of diagnostic criteria for Traumatic Grief until now, there is little data to support a causative relationship. Still, it is conceivable, for example, that Traumatic Grief might predispose to a Major Depressive Episode or that a Major Depressive Episode, existing before bereavement, might predispose to Traumatic Grief. One analysis of these alternative structural models in elderly widows indicated that the pathway of Major Depression predisposing to Traumatic Grief fit the data better (Prigerson et al., 1996a). Whatever the relationship between Traumatic Grief and other types of coexisting psychopathology, the most fundamental implication of the potential comorbidity during bereavement is this: Having diagnosed one disorder, it is essential to always look for a second or even third diagnosis as the chances are good for finding comorbidity.

This chapter reviews what is known about the rates, natural history, and degree of overlap of several psychiatric disorders during bereavement.

Major Depressive Disorder

Depressive symptoms are ubiquitous and Major Depressive Episodes are common during bereavement. Clayton and colleagues observed depressive episodes in 45% of acutely bereaved spouses at some time during the first year of bereavement (Bornstein et al., 1973). While many of these depressive syndromes resolved on their own during the first year of bereavement, 17% of the bereaved persons had a persistent depressive syndrome starting in the first month after the death and lasting throughout the first year. We now know that some depressive syndromes extend considerably beyond one year. For example, 25 months after bereavement, Zisook and colleagues observed a 14% prevalence of depressive syndromes in mid-life and elderly bereaved spouses (Zisook, Shuchter, & Sledge, 1994). This 25-month prevalence rate is about three times higher than that observed in the general population.

The degree of comorbidity of Major Depressive Episodes and Traumatic Grief, by comparison with other possible disorders that occur during bereavement, may be the greatest. In a small study, using diagnostic criteria for pathologic grief that were closely related to the consensus criteria, 94% of persons with pathologic grief also had a diagnosis of Major Depression at the time of assessment, which occurred 6 to 13 months into bereavement (Kim & Jacobs, 1991). Conversely, 80% of persons who met criteria for Major Depression also met criteria for pathologic grief. These are probably exaggerated figures as the sample for study was referred because of problems with bereavement, making it more likely that these referrals would have comorbidity. In contrast, in an analysis of comorbid caseness of Major Depression and Traumatic Grief using the Kappa statistic, which corrects for chance, a much lower rate of overlap (Kappa = .54) was found (Prigerson et al., 1995). The latter data suggest, therefore, that overlap between Major Depression and Traumatic Grief, although important to appreciate, appears to be limited. To provide a more precise understanding, these estimates, and those below for the other disorders, need verification in a large sample using consensus, diagnostic criteria for Traumatic Grief.

Interestingly, one analysis of comorbid, syndromal level, Traumatic Grief symptoms and major depression, while documenting a main effect for each disorder, does not show an increased relative risk of suicidal ideation if a person has both disorders (Prigerson, H. G., unpublished data). This finding is one example of when comorbidity may not complicate or aggravate symptoms, contrary to the assumption articulated in the introduction to this chapter that comorbidity can aggravate the symptoms of each disorder. While limited to just this symptom and based only on one analysis, this finding emphasizes the need to check our clinical assumptions in systematic, empirical studies, which the availability of consensus diagnostic criteria makes possible.

Despite the limitations of the available data, it is safe to say that it is important to look for Major Depression when a diagnosis of Traumatic Grief is made and vice versa. Additionally, to the extent that the treatments for each disorder differ, it is important to address both treatment tasks and monitor both domains of symptoms. The case example below illustrates some of the ideas introduced in this section.

Panic Disorder and Generalized Anxiety Disorder

Anxious symptoms are also common during acute bereavement (Clayton, 1990) and do not diminish in intensity between 2 and 7 months after a death (Zisook, Schneider, & Shuchter, 1990b). In the only study that provides rates of anxiety disorders during bereavement, 6.3% of bereaved adults at 6 months and 13% at 12 months met criteria for Panic Disorder. For Generalized Anxiety Disorder, 23% met criteria at 6 months and 39% at 12 months (Jacobs et al., 1990). The only risk factor identified for these disorders was a past personal history of anxiety disorders. There are no data on the occurrence of anxiety disorders during or after the second year of bereavement, or on the course of anxiety syndromes during bereavement.

The same study discussed above about comorbidity of Major Depression also reported on the rates of anxiety disorders during bereavement (Kim & Jacobs, 1991). In this study of middle aged, bereaved spouses who met criteria for pathologic grief, 36% also had the diagnosis of Panic Disorder, and 82% had the diagnosis of Generalized Anxiety Disorder. Conversely, 80% of those with Panic Disorder and 69% of those with Generalized Anxiety Disorder also met criteria for pathologic grief.

Thus, as was the case in the discussion of comorbid Major Depression above, when a diagnosis of Traumatic Grief is made, it is important to look for coexisting anxiety disorders. And, to the extent that the treatments for each disorder differ, it is important to address both treatment tasks and monitor both domains of symptoms.

Post-traumatic Stress Disorder

One study, using self-report measures, has systematically documented traumatic symptoms during acute bereavement. The sample was 128 widowed persons whose marital partners died from multiple causes. The classification of cause of death included unexpected, often sudden deaths in 52% of the sample and violent deaths in 6% (Schut et al., 1991). The presence of intrusive and avoidant traumatic symptoms was very common, occurring in 60% to 80% of the sample, depending on when they were assessed. Assessment took place at 4 points over 25 months of follow-up. Twenty to 31% of the sample met criteria for Post-traumatic

Stress Disorder, depending on the point of assessment over the 25 months. Nine percent carried the diagnosis of PTSD throughout all 4 assessments over the 25 months of follow-up. The traumatic symptoms were significantly associated with not having anticipated the loss and not having taken leave of the person who died. The symptoms were more likely to occur in young men. Traumatic syndromes, and indeed the diagnosis of PTSD in the 9% of widowed persons who met criteria throughout the entire 25 months of follow up, were not associated with traumatic and unnatural causes of death.

Another study from the epidemiologic literature provides information on the rates of PTSD in the community after a death. In a representative sample of 18- to 45-year-old persons living in an urban community, sudden, unexpected death of a close friend or relative, above and beyond other traumatic events occurring to others, contributed a large proportion of PTSD cases (31%) to the overall prevalence of PTSD in the community. This was true because of the high, lifetime prevalence rate of sudden, unexpected deaths in the population (60%) and a moderate conditional risk of PTSD if a sudden, unexpected death occurred (14.3%). Note that these findings are consistent with the observations in the previous study that PTSD can occur after sudden, unexpected deaths. Neither of the two studies just discussed document or comment on the clinical presumption that PTSD also occurs after violent deaths.

Not many data are available to provide information on the degree of comorbidity between Traumatic Grief and Post-traumatic Stress Disorder. Although the authors of the bereavement study described above acknowledge that PTSD and pathologic grief are separate diagnostic entities and hypothesize partial overlap, they do not present data on these questions (Schut et al., 1991). One report using a Kappa statistic for comorbidity of Traumatic Grief and PTSD, found the overlap of Traumatic Grief and PTSD caseness was quite low (Kappa = .27) (Prigerson & Jacobs, in press). In another study of young persons exposed to a teen suicide, the authors found only 34% agreement (Phi Coefficient) between caseness for Traumatic Grief and the diagnosis of PTSD (Prigerson, H. G., unpublished data). Thus, overlap between Traumatic Grief and Post-traumatic Stress Disorder appears to be limited.

When Traumatic Grief and Post-traumatic Stress Disorder are comorbid, it is important to address the treatment implications of both and monitor both domains of symptoms, as noted above for Major Depression and anxiety disorders. In addition, several authors have emphasized the higher priority of treating the PTSD before treating Traumatic Grief (Rynearson et al., 1993; Rynearson, 1996; Raphael et al., 1993); Pynoos & Nader, 1993; Rando, 1993). This treatment assumption, which is based on clinical experience and needs systematic testing, is discussed more in chapter 6. Some of the issues under discussion in this section are illustrated in the case example below.

Alcohol Abuse

On average, bereaved persons increase their consumption of alcohol (Clayton & Darvish, 1979; Thompson, Breckenridge, Gallagher, & Peterson, 1984; Zisook et al., 1990a). On the other hand, in controlled studies, the difference in alcohol consumption between bereaved persons and controls is statistically nonsignificant (Kasl, Ostfeld, Berkman, & Jacobs, 1987), or the change in consumption over the first year of bereavement, despite being statistically significant, is not clinically impressive, going from 1.8 to 2.2 drinks per day (Zisook et al., 1990a). One study has found higher alcohol consumption among persons with high scores on Traumatic Grief symptoms (Prigerson et al., 1997). The strongest evidence for an increased risk of hazardous alcohol consumption during bereavement comes from an Australian controlled study of 57 elderly widowers in the city of Brisbane (Byrne, 1995). The use of alcohol included both greater frequency of use and greater quantity of consumption in bereaved men with comparison to married men. In particular, this appeared to a problem among bereaved men who had previously established patterns of drinking.

No data are available on the rates of comorbid Traumatic Grief and alcohol abuse.

Assuming that the observation of increased alcohol abuse among elderly widowers in Australia holds true for American society, particular attention ought to be paid to this type of potentially comorbid complication in this group of bereaved persons.

Risk of suicide

There is evidence for an elevated risk of suicidal gestures (Birtchnell, 1970) and successful suicide following the death of a spouse or a parent (Bock & Weber, 1972; Bunch 1972; Bunch, Barraclough, Nelson, & Sainsbury, 1971; MacMahon and Pugh, 1965; Murphy, Armstrong, Hermele, Fischer, & Clendenin, 1979; Stein & Susser, 1969). In comparison to the general, bereaved population the risk is higher among bereaved persons who seek help (Bunch, 1972), young widows (Stein & Susser, 1969) and elderly widowers (Bock & Webber, 1972; MacMahon & Pugh, 1965). Adult men who lose their mother may be a particularly vulnerable group (Bunch et al., 1971). Risk factors for suicide during bereavement also include a past history of treatment for Major Depression, past suicidal gestures, absence of support from relatives during bereavement, living alone after the death, alcohol abuse, agitated depressive symptoms, and perhaps multiple losses (Bunch, 1972; Murphy et al., 1979; Birtchnell, 1970; Gregory, 1994). These risk factors can be fortified with risk factors from general practice in the clinic, including the existence of medical comorbidity, a family history of suicide, pervasive despair, and a feasible, lethal plan of suicide such as possession of a gun.

Only one study has addressed the question of whether the risk of suicide is higher among bereaved persons who have Traumatic Grief. Controlling for depression, high symptom scores for Traumatic Grief were significantly correlated with higher suicidality, measured by the Kovacs Scale (Prigerson, H. G., unpublished data).

Bereavement and Schizophrenic Disorder

Although a common presumption in the clinic is that bereavement is particularly stressful for persons with Schizophrenic Disorders, no data are available in the literature to support the idea of a high risk of Traumatic Grief or other complications of bereavement for schizophrenic patients. Furthermore, despite some data on stress and Schizophrenic Disorder, bereavement specifically is not a known risk factor for the onset or relapse of Schizophrenic Disorders. The assumption that persons with a Schizophrenic Disorder might run a high risk of developing Traumatic Grief or other clinical complications after the death of a parent or anyone who has served as a custodian or in other ways has been instrumental and supportive in their lives, needs systematic testing.

Generally, there is a tendency to shield patients with Schizophrenic Disorder from the funeral of significant others, to prophylactically increase the dosage of antipsychotic drugs, and sometimes to preemptively hospitalize them after the death of a significant other. There is no empirical basis for these practices, and there are the risks of adverse effects of higher dosage and the occurrence of symptomatic regression during hospitalization. While we await more data, I recommend that patients with Schizophrenic Disorders be treated with common sense and sympathy like any other person during bereavement. To practice safely, clinicians can provide more intensive monitoring of the course of the schizophrenic illness and vigilance for the emergence of complications of bereavement in persons with Schizophrenic Disorder after the death of a significant other. Schizophrenic patients should be supported in their personal decisions about whether to attend the funeral or not, with a bias in my opinion towards encouraging them to do so if they can.

☐ Traumatic Grief: Is it Old Wine in a New Bottle?

High rates of comorbidity of psychiatric disorders during bereavement raise a cogent question about whether the diagnosis of Traumatic Grief adds anything to our understanding of (or to our powers to treat) psychopathology that occurs during bereavement. A skeptic would argue the negative position on this question and cite primarily the rates of comorbidity as evidence. I argue that Traumatic Grief is different and distinct from other disorders and not simply another way of packaging the same symptoms. There are several studies, including the comorbidity data, and an argument rooted in treatment that support this affirmative position.

Recently in a series of factor analyses, Prigerson and colleagues have distinguished symptoms of Traumatic Grief from those of depression and anxiety (Prigerson et al., 1995; Prigerson et al., 1996b). In addition, they have shown that traumatic grief, depression, and anxiety factors differentially predict subsequent symptoms. These data were cited in chapter 2 to support the development of Traumatic Grief as a new diagnostic entity. Also, in a study from the same group, the evolution over time of pathologic grief symptoms (a flat trajectory) measured by the Texas Revised Inventory of Grief followed a different course from symptoms of depression (improved trajectory) measured by the Hamilton Depression Rating Scale in a sample of elderly, bereaved persons treated with nortriptylene (Pasternak et al., 1993). Furthermore, studies of comorbidity (discussed above) have found substantially incomplete overlap in the occurrence of pathologic grief, Major Depression, Panic Disorder, and Generalized Anxiety Disorder during acute bereavement (Kim & Jacobs, 1991). Finally, a recent sleep study of persons with high scores on Traumatic Grief differentiated depression from Traumatic Grief, which did not entail the changes of EEG sleep physiology seen in Major Depression (McDermott, Prigerson, & Reynolds, 1997).

In addition to these studies, there is suggestive evidence that the treatment of Traumatic Grief may be improved with the use of specific interventions for it. Two, small, open psychotropic drug trials, one of desipramine and another of nortriptyline, noted less robust improvement in separation distress than in depressive symptoms (Jacobs, Nelson, & Zisook, 1987; Pasternak et al., 1991), and another open, uncontrolled trial using paroxetine, reported equal efficacy for the symptoms of Traumatic Grief and depressive symptoms (Zygmont et al., 1998). In addition, several clinical experts have recommended specific psychotherapies for Traumatic Grief for the purpose of optimal intervention after a death (Worden, 1982; Horowitz et al., 1984; Zisook & Shuchter, 1996; Jacobs &

Prigerson, 1996; Rynearson, 1996). Treatment studies such as these, which are reviewed more in the next chapter, offer at best only indirect evidence of the unique nature of Traumatic Grief. Still, they may hold important leads to understanding the nature of the disorder.

I conclude that Traumatic Grief is not just an alternate way of describing Major Depressions, anxiety disorders, and Post-traumatic Stress Disorders. Even if it were, if the diagnosis of Traumatic Grief focused more precisely on the nature of the disorder, its recognition, and its treatment, it would be an improvement in nosology and desirable for the purposes of improving our understanding and powers to intervene.

☐ Diagnosis of a Comorbid Disorder During Bereavement: Special Considerations

The diagnosis of comorbid disorders during bereavement involves some special considerations. While the same diagnostic criteria used in the general psychiatric clinic apply in the circumstances of bereavement, there are some bereavement specific guidelines for diagnosis.

The best developed example of these special considerations is the diagnosis of a Major Depressive Episode during bereavement. The DSM-IV provides the following guidelines for the diagnosis of a Major Depressive Episode during bereavement (Diagnostic and Statistical Manual, 4th ed., 1994). It recommends that physicians diagnose Major Depression if 1) a depressive syndrome is present for more than 2 months after a loss or 2) a depressive syndrome includes marked functional impairment, morbid preoccupation with worthlessness, morbid guilt, suicidal ideation, psychotic symptoms, or psychomotor retardation. The symptoms in the second part of the guideline reflect not only specific qualities of the syndrome but also the severity of the syndrome. Note the difference from standard criteria in duration of the syndrome required for diagnosis of a Major Depressive Episode during bereavement (2 months versus 2 weeks). Also, note the either/or grammar. That is, either prolonged duration or the DSM-IV flagged symptoms justify the diagnosis of a Major Depressive Episode in the circumstances of bereavement. Thus, the diagnosis of a Major Depressive Episode during bereavement is based not only on the application of standard criteria for diagnosis used in the general psychiatric clinic but also on certain, flagged symptoms, the severity of the syndrome, or the course of the Major Depressive Episode.

DSM-IV does not discuss the occurrence of anxiety disorders and Post-traumatic Stress Disorders during bereavement, nor have these disorders been the focus of studies and clinical experience during bereavement to the extent of Major Depressive Disorder. Therefore, it is difficult to discuss special considerations for bereavement-specific diagnosis of them in the same detail. Nevertheless, the general principles embodied in the discussion of depressive disorders during bereavement probably apply, particularly to the anxiety disorders. These include the need to develop an understanding of the importance of specific symptoms, the severity of the syndrome, and the duration of the syndrome when it occurs in the circumstances of bereavement.

☐ Clinical Examples

Mrs. C.: An Example of a Major Depressive Episode and Traumatic Grief

Mrs. C., a 43-year-old married mother of 2 children, presented for evaluation 22 months after her mother's death. Her father had died in an automobile accident when she was 13. Her grief over the death of her mother started intensely in the first month of bereavement and had continued without relief. Her chief complaint was "I can't get over my mother's death" and "I'm depressed." She feared that her symptoms were causing serious marital difficulties and interfered with her ability to care for her children. She met criteria for a Major Depressive Episode with symptoms that included sad mood, crying, guilt over not loving her husband whom she viewed as nonsupportive since her mother's death, sleep continuity disturbance, chronic fatigue, loss of interest in social activities, excessive appetite, and a weight gain of 15 pounds. She had suicidal ruminations, which were most intense immediately after the death of her mother and recurred infrequently in dreams of a peaceful death relieving her of all her distress and worries. After a false start on desipramine which caused severe sweating, and then 1 week on amitriptyline, she noticed initial relief of her depressive symptoms that consolidated and progressed over the next few weeks.

Two weeks after starting antidepressant treatment, she feared she was relapsing. She had become totally preoccupied with her deceased mother and longed to have her back. This yearning appeared ambivalent as she described intense anger over her mother's death and at her mother for failing to support her after the death of her father years before. The second anniversary of her mother's death loomed as a nemesis which she wanted to avoid. She needed active encouragement to face the question of what she would do to observe the anniversary. She felt as if she wanted to build a wall around herself, which was reflected in her sense of detachment and emotional unresponsiveness to her husband and children. She was self-critical for not being able to handle her feelings and problems better and "wallowing in self-pity," as her mother would have seen it, corresponding to an inner voice of her mother's telling her to "forget about me." This self-critical attitude was reminiscent of the attitude of her stoic, critical mother after the death of her father, and seemed to be an example of identification with a harmful behavior related to her mother. After careful examination of this history, it became clear that she was experiencing an intensification of separation distress and ambivalent relationship issues, and this accounted for her concern about relapse. Furthermore, most of the symptoms were consistent with the grief she reported in the early stages of her bereavement and appeared to be mostly present but also waxed and waned over several months. These symptoms were addressed in ongoing psychotherapy, and she continued to experience relief from her depression.

This bereaved, adult daughter met criteria for a Major Depressive Episode and, eventually, for Traumatic Grief, as the symptoms of separation distress intensified during treatment of the depression. In the course of treatment of the Major Depression, there was an interesting interplay of the depressive symptoms with the symptoms of Traumatic Grief. Unless the clinician was able to appreciate the distinctions between depression and grief and carefully evaluate the symptoms of relapse, there was a risk of jumping to false conclusions about the need to switch antidepressants, whereas in this case the so-called relapse was managed easily and reassuringly by psychoeducation. Also, it seemed as if the treatment of the Major Depressive Episode facilitated this woman's ability to experience and cope with her grief.

Mr. D.: An example of Post-traumatic Stress Disorder and Traumatic Grief

Mr. D. was a 45-year-old businessman whose 26-year-old, newly married daughter was assaulted and murdered by a stranger who was high on drugs. The father presented for evaluation one year after the death. His chief complaint was "confusion," by which he meant the conflict between the intense grief (separation distress) and trauma that he experienced. He was tortured by intrusive images of his daughter's death that flooded him repeatedly and left him feeling helpless, violated, and vengeful. He said he felt like a failure. It was my impression that the traumatic replay overshadowed his grief. His violent fantasies towards the murderer, including occasional lurking behavior around the prison where the murderer was housed, concerned his family. He himself feared that he would lose control of his murderous rage and do something "crazy," perhaps in connection with a court appearance. His "confusion" was compounded by the failure of the criminal justice system to bring the alleged murderer, who was exploring an insanity plea, to justice promptly and efficiently. His basic assumptions about himself and his family life in a safe, predictable, and just world were violently shaken. He viewed his environment as threatening, hostile, and untrustworthy. He felt "on edge" and a need to prowl this environment, particularly parts of the criminal justice system. He was highly aroused and hypervigilant, as he scanned the environment for the next calamity that would befall him. He described a disruption of normal sleep patterns, was unable to rest, and felt chronically fatigued. In the early mornings, he felt agitated to the point of feeling like screaming. He was unable to concentrate and lost interest in athletics and social activities. He reported intermittent depressive symptoms during the first year of bereavement and for the month prior to his evaluation he met criteria for Major Depression. In addition, he was intensely preoccupied, yearned, and longed to have his daughter back. His world view was shattered by the nightmarish death of his daughter. He tried to cope with his intense panoply of symptoms by pacing himself through the work day, volunteering work at local agencies, and avoiding reminders. He felt as if his coping efforts were constantly overwhelmed.

This bereaved father, whose daughter's death was conspicuously violent and untimely, met criteria for the diagnosis of Post-traumatic Stress Disorder. This was true for most of the first year of bereavement. At the time of evaluation, he also met all the criteria for Traumatic Grief. One year after the death he also met criteria for Major Depression, including intermittent suicidal ruminations.

His treatment focused on the traumatic symptoms as these overshadowed everything else, and he needed help in coping with them. In addition, his depressive syndrome was treated with desipramine. As a clinical relationship developed and as the antidepressant provided relief, he seemed progressively able to focus on his intense separation feelings.

☐ Conclusion

This chapter discusses several psychiatric disorders that are observed during bereavement, occur at a higher rate than usual during bereavement, and can be comorbid disorders with Traumatic Grief. The most fundamental implication of this discussion of comorbidity is that, having made the diagnosis of Traumatic Grief, or the diagnosis of any other psychiatric disorder during acute bereavement, it is essential to consider whether psychiatric comorbidity exists. Some bereavement specific considerations for the diagnosis of comorbid disorders are discussed. Another important implication of comorbidity is the need to monitor both domains of symptoms and consider the effects of treatment on both.

☐ References

Birtchnell, J. (1970). The relationship between attempted suicide, depression and parent death. *British Journal of Psychiatry, 116,* 307–313.

Bock, E. W., & Webber, I. L. (1972). Suicide among the elderly: Isolating widowhood and mitigating alternatives. *Journal of Marriage and the Family, 8,* 24–31.

Bornstein, P. C., Clayton, P. J., Halikas, J. A., Maurice, W. L., & Robins, E. (1973). The depression of widowhood after thirteen months. *British Journal of Psychiatry, 122,* 561–566.

Bunch, J., Barraclough, B. M., Nelson, B., & Sainsbury, P. (1971). Suicide following death of parents. *Social Psychiatry, 6,* 193–199.

Bunch, J. (1972). Recent bereavement in relation to suicide. *Journal of Psychosomatic Research, 16,* 361–366.

Byrne, G. J. A. (1995). Aging: Opportunities for preventive intervention. In B. Raphael, & G. D. Burrows, (Eds.), *Handbook of Studies on Preventive Psychiatry* (chapter 9). Amsterdam: Elsevier.

Clayton, P. J. (1990). Bereavement and depression. *Journal of Clinical Psychiatry, 51,* 34–38.

Clayton, P. J., & Darvish, H. S. (1979). Course of depressive symptoms following the stress of bereavement. In J. E. Barrett, R. M. Rose, & G. L. Kleman, (Eds.), *Stress and Mental Disorder* (pp. 121–136). New York: Raven Press.

Diagnostic and Statistical Manual of Mental Disorders (4th ed.). (1994). Washington, DC: American Psychiatric Press, Inc.

Gregory, R. J. (1994). Grief and loss among Eskimos attempting suicide in western Alaska. *American Journal of Psychiatry, 151,* 1815–1816.

Horowitz, M. J.,. Marmar, C., Weiss, D. S., DeWitt, K., Rosenbaum, R. (1984). Brief psychotherapy of bereavement reactions: The relationship of process to outcome. *Archives of General Psychiatry, 41,* 438–448.

Jacobs, S. C., Nelson, J. C., Zisook, S. (1987). Treating depressions of bereavement with antidepressants: A pilot study. *Psychiatric Clinics of North America, 10,* 501–510.

Jacobs, S. C., Hansen, F. F., Berkman, L., Kasl, S., Ostfeld, A. (1989). Depressions of bereavement. *Comprehensive Psychiatry, 30,* 218–224.

Jacobs, S. C., Hanson, F., Kasl, S. V., Ostfeld, A. M., Berkman, L., & Kim, K. (1990). Anxiety disorders during acute bereavement: Risk and risk factors. *Journal of Clinical Psychiatry, 51,* 269–274.

Jacobs, S., & Prigerson, H. G. (1996). Problem focused, integrated psychotherapy for complicated grief. *In Session: Psychotherapy in Practice, 2,* 21–30.

Kasl, S. V., Ostfeld, A. M., Berkman, L. F., & Jacobs, S. C. (1987). Stress and alcohol consumption: The role of selected social and environmental factors. In E. Gottheil, K. A. Druley, S. Pashko, & S. P. Weinstein, (Eds.), *Stress and addiction.* (pp. 40–60). New York: Brunner Mazel.

Kim, K., & Jacobs, S. C. (1991). Pathologic grief and its relationship to other psychiatric disorders. *Journal of Affective Disorders, 21,* 257–263.

MacMahon, B., & Pugh, T. F. (1965). Suicide in the widowed. *American Journal of Epidemiology, 81*, 23–31.

McDermott, O., Prigerson, H. G., & Reynolds, C. F. (1997). EEG sleep in complicated grief and bereavement-related depression: A preliminary report. *Biological Psychiatry, 41*, 710–716.

Murphy, G. E., Armstrong, M. D., Hermele, S. L., Fischer, J. R., & Clendenin, W. W. (1979). Suicide and alcoholism. *Archives of General Psychiatry, 36*, 65–69.

Pasternak, R. E., Reynolds, C. F., Schlernitzauer, M., Hoch, C. C., Bugsse, D. J., Houck, P. R., & Perel, J. M. (1991). Acute open-trial nortriptyline therapy of bereavement-related depression in late life. *Journal of Clinical Psychiatry, 52*, 307–310.

Pasternak, R. E., Reynolds, C. F., Frank, E., Miller, M. D., Houck, P. R., Schlernitzauer, M., Prigerson, H. G., & Kupfer, D. J. (1993). The temporal course of depressive symptoms and grief intensity in late life spousal bereavement. *Depression, 1*, 45–49.

Prigerson, H. G., Frank, E., Kasl, S. V., Reynolds, C. F., Anderson, B., Zubenko, G. S., Houck, P. R., George, C. J., & Kupfer, D. J. (1995). Complicated grief and bereavement-related depression as distinct disorders: Preliminary empirical validation in elderly bereaved spouses. *American Journal of Psychiatry, 152*, 22–30.

Prigerson, H. G., Shear, M. K., Newsom, J., Frank, E., Reynolds, C. F., Houck, P. R., Bierhals, A. J., Kupfer, D. J., Maciejewski, P. K. (1996a). Anxiety among widowed elders: Is it distinct from depression and grief. *Anxiety, 2*, 1–12.

Prigerson, H. G., Bierhals, A. J., Kasl, S. V., Reynolds, C. F., Shear, M. K., Newsom, J. T., Jacobs, S. C. (1996b). Complicated grief as a distinct disorder from bereavement-related depression and anxiety: A replication study. *The American Journal of Psychiatry, 153*, 1484–1486.

Prigerson, H. G., Bierhals, A. J., Kasl, S. V., Reynolds, C. F., Shear, M. K., Day, N., Beery, L. C., Newsom, J. T., & Jacobs, S. (1997). Traumatic grief as a risk factor for mental and physical morbidity. *American Journal of Psychiatry, 154*, 617–623.

Prigerson, H. G., Beery, L. C., Bridge, J., Rosenheck, R. A., Maciejewski, P. K., Kupfer, D. J., & Brent, D. (in press). Traumatic grief as a risk factor for suicidal ideation among young adults. *American Journal of Psychiatry.*

Prigerson, H. G., Shear, M. K., Jacobs, S. C., Reynolds, C. F., Maciejewski, P. K., Pilkonis, P., Wortman, C., Williams, J. B. W., Widiger, T. A., Davidson, J., Frank, E., Kupfer, D. J., Zisook, S. (in press). Consensus criteria for traumatic grief: A preliminary empirical test. *British Journal of Psychiatry.*

Prigerson, H. G., & Jacobs, S. C. (in press). Diagnostic criteria for traumatic grief: Conceptual issues, critical appraisal, and an empirical test. In M. S. Stroebe, W. Stroebe, R. O. Hansson, & H. Schut, (Eds.), *New handbook of bereavement: Consequences, coping and care.* Washington, DC: American Psychological Association Press.

Pynoos, R. S., & Nader, K. (1993). Issues in the treatment of post traumatic stress in children and adolescents. In J. P. Wilson, & B. Raphael, (Eds.), *The international handbook of traumatic stress syndromes.* (pp. 535–549). New York: Plenum Press.

Rando, T. A. (1993). *Treatment of complicated mourning.* Champaign, IL: Research Press.

Raphael, B., Middleton, W., Martinek, N., & Misso, V. (1993). Counseling and therapy of the bereaved. In M. S. Stroebe, W. Stroebe, R. O. Hansson, (Eds.), *Handbook of bereavement: Theory, research and intervention.* (pp. 427–453). Cambridge, England: Cambridge University Press.

Rynearson, E. K. (1987). Psychotherapy of pathologic grief. *Psychiatric Clinics of North America, 10*, 487–499.

Rynearson, E. K., & McCreery, J. M. (1993). Bereavement after homicide: A synergism of trauma and loss. *American Journal of Psychiatry, 150*, 258–261.

Rynearson, E. K. (1996). Psychotherapy of bereavement after homicide: Be offensive. *In Sessions: Psychotherapy in Practice, 2*, 47–57.

Schut, H. A. W., de Keijser, J., van den Bout, J., & Dijhuis, J. H. (1991). Post-traumatic symptoms in the first year of conjugal bereavement. *Anxiety Research, 4,* 225–234.

Stein, Z., Susser, M. (1969). Widowhood and mental illness. *British Journal of Preventive and Social Medicine, 23,* 106–110.

Thompson, L., Breckenridge, J., Gallagher, D., & Peterson, J. (1984). Effects of bereavement on self-perceptions of physical health in elderly widows and widowers. *Journal of Gerontology, 39,* 309–314.

Worden, J. W. (1982). *Grief counseling and grief therapy: A handbook for the mental health practitioner.* New York: Springer.

Zisook, S., Shuchter, S. R., & Mulvilhill, M. (1990a). Alcohol, cigarette, and medication use during the first year of widowhood. *Psychiatric Annals, 20,* 318–326.

Zisook, S., Schneider, D., & Shuchter, S. R. (1990b). Anxiety and bereavement. *Psychiatric Medicine, 8,* 83–96.

Zisook, S., Shuchter, S. R. (1991). Depression through the first year after the death of a spouse. *American Journal of Psychiatry, 148,* 1346–1352.

Zisook, S., & Shuchter, S. R. (1993). Uncomplicated bereavement. *Journal of Clinical Psychiatry, 54,* 365–372.

Zisook, S., & Shuchter, S. R. (1996). Psychotherapy of the depressions in spousal bereavement. *In Session: Psychotherapy in Practice, 2,* 31–45.

Zisook, S., Shuchter, S. R., & Sledge, P. (1994). Diagnostic considerations in depression associated with late-life bereavement. In *Diagnosis and treatment of depression in the elderly: Results of the NIH consensus development conference.* Washington, DC: American Psychiatric Press.

Zygmont, M., Prigerson, H. G., Houck, P. R., Miller, M. D., Shear, M. K., Jacobs, S., Reynolds, C. F. III (1998). A post-hoc comparison of paroxetine and nortriptyline for symptoms of traumatic grief. *The Journal of Clinical Psychiatry, 59,* 241–255.

Treatment of Traumatic Grief

This chapter reviews the evidence for specific or potentially specific treatments of Traumatic Grief. It also sets the stage, along with chapter 3 on diagnosis, for the development of a diagnosis/treatment algorithm in chapter 6. Before reviewing recent studies that create a foundation for treating Traumatic Grief, it is useful to return to a basic philosophical question about treatment. I place emphasis on this philosophical issue as I have found that it can interfere with treatment decisions if it is not explicitly addressed by each clinician.

☐ A Philosophy of Treatment

A preliminary task is to address a philosophical question about the treatment of Traumatic Grief, or any of the other clinical complications of bereavement for that matter. Focusing more specifically on Traumatic Grief, the question is whether it is wise to treat Traumatic Grief under any conditions or circumstances. Strong philosophical attitudes prevail in the medical community and in society at large to the effect that we should not "medicalize" or interfere with the natural process of grief. Moreover, as part of medical education, all physicians, and many other clinicians, are taught the professional dictum of "primum non nocere." The admonition to "first, do no harm" lends itself to treatment conservatism, if not nihilism, in the case of Traumatic Grief. These concerns must be taken seriously.

Given the enormous advances in psychiatric research and the potential for more research, I believe the debate about whether to treat Traumatic Grief should hinge on scientific studies. Therefore, I have anchored the position developed in this book in scientific studies that define and validate the syndrome of Traumatic Grief and its evidence-based treatment, which will be reviewed below. In addition to scientific evidence, philosophical arguments serve as a counterpoint to entrenched cultural attitudes against treatment during bereavement. For example, it is reasonable to ask how much a bereaved person needs to suffer. It is also reasonable to consider the responsibility of professionals to alleviate excessive pain and to attenuate, if not prevent, clinical complications.

The metaphor of an injury with subsequent inflammation and the risk of abscess formation is useful for loss and grief (Engel, 1961). The analogy provides concepts for understanding how knowledge of the normal physiology of attachment behavior and affiliation can be applied to monitor the natural process of grief (inflammation) after a loss (injury). In addition, it illustrates how psychotropic and psychotherapeutic interventions (medical treatments) can be used to help bereaved persons with the clinical complication of Traumatic Grief (superimposed abscess development). The aim is to accomplish all this while facilitating overall healing without compromising a normal behavioral and physiologic process.

The analogy of obstetrical care is equally illuminating. Obstetricians and other professional caregivers contribute to a reduction in complications, alleviate unnecessary pain and suffering, and provide expert judgment and management during the natural process of childbirth.

While I recommend resolution of these issues on the side of an open minded, scientific approach, it is important that clinicians think through and resolve these issues for themselves. Having flagged these philosophical questions, this chapter now turns to a review of systematic studies of both psychopharmacologic and psychotherapeutic treatments of Traumatic Grief or related disorders.

☐ Overview of Treatment

There are no randomized, controlled, clinical trials of treatment for Traumatic Grief, as it has emerged too recently as an entity. Still, I believe that literature exists that has a bearing on the treatment of Traumatic Grief. In short, I conceive of Traumatic Grief as an adult type of Separation Anxiety Disorder. The rationale for this assumption is based on the natural and historical relationship of Traumatic Grief to Separation Anxiety

Disorder, explained in chapter 2. Accordingly, I will review studies of the treatment of Separation Anxiety Disorder in children and the treatment of pathologic grief in adults. Also, given the traumatic elements of Traumatic Grief, I briefly review treatments developed for Post-traumatic Stress Disorder on the assumption that these studies can provide leads for the treatment of Traumatic Grief. As a final note, it is important to emphasize that the conclusions derived from such a review will need confirmation from systematic study.

☐ Psychopharmacology

Drug Treatment of Separation Anxiety Disorder in Children and Adolescents

The literature on the drug treatment of Separation Anxiety Disorder in children and adolescents contains several controlled studies of tricyclic antidepressants, a few open trials of a selective serotonin reuptake inhibitor, and several studies of benzodiazepines including one controlled trial. Based on the review, the selective serotonin reuptake inhibitors emerge as the most promising treatment.

There are four placebo controlled trials of tricyclic antidepressants that provide mixed results and leave only a suggestion that tricyclics may be helpful in relieving symptoms of Separation Anxiety Disorder in children. As early study reporting significant benefit for school phobia from treatment with imipramine (Gittelman and Klein, 1971) was not replicated either by the same group in a subsequent study of a sample of 21 children with Separation Anxiety Disorder (Klein, Koplewitz, & Kanner, 1992) or another group (Bernstein, Garfinkel, & Borchardt, 1990). Therefore, the use of tricyclics for treating Separation Anxiety Disorder in children remains an open question and has been overtaken for the most part by the introduction of selective serotonin reuptake inhibitors.

Two open trials of fluoxetine, involving a total of 37 children with anxiety disorders, suggest the efficacy of fluoxetine, and perhaps other selective serotonin reuptake inhibitors, for separation anxiety disorder (Birmaher et al., 1994; Fairbanks et al., 1997). Because these results are consistent with the small, open trial by Zygmont and colleagues in adults with Traumatic Grief (Zygmont et al., 1998) they are described next.

Birmaher and colleagues studied fluoxetine treatment of 21 children in the age range of 11 and 17 (Birmaher et al., 1994). The sample included 11 males and 10 females. Ten of the children had Separation Anxiety Disorder in conjunction with overanxious disorder or social phobia, or both. Children with Major Depression were excluded. The mean fluoxetine dose was 25.7 milligrams per day. The study noted significant reductions in anxious and depressive symptoms that began 6 to 8 weeks after treatment began. Only one child showed no change. The number of disorders a child had did not affect response to the treatment. After controlling for initial depression scores and for change in depression scores over treatment, fluoxetine still produced a significant decrease in anxiety scores, suggesting improvement in symptoms of anxiety was independent of the presence of depressive symptoms. There were no adverse reactions, and side effects such as headache, nausea, insomnia, and anorexia were mild and transient.

In another open trial, Fairbanks and colleagues studied fluoxetine in 16 children with mixed anxiety disorders following nonresponse to psychotherapy (Fairbanks et al., 1997). The sample included 8 boys and 8 girls, ranging from 9 to 18 years of age. Ten children had Separation Anxiety Disorder. Those with Major Depression were excluded. The period of active treatment was 9 weeks and employed flexible dosing within different guidelines for children and adolescents. The mean fluoxetine dose for 9 to 12 year olds was 24 milligrams ($\pm$ 8.9). For 12 to 18 year olds, it was 40 milligrams ($\pm$ 17.9). Children with multiple diagnoses required a significantly higher dose. Of the 10 children treated for Separation Anxiety Disorder, all were rated as improved or much improved at the end of treatment. Four were rated as improved (significant reduction in symptoms) and 6 were rated as much improved (significant reduction of symptoms as well as enhanced social or school functioning). Seven of the 10 children with Separation Anxiety Disorder no longer met criteria for diagnosis after treatment. Signs of improvement took an average of 5 weeks to emerge. Age did not affect response to treatment. Among the anxiety disorders of childhood, Separation Anxiety Disorder had the best response to treatment. No adverse effects of treatment were noted.

Several small, open trials of benzodiazepines including chlordiaepoxide, clonazepan, and alprazolam over many years suggest they might be effective in treating separation anxiety in children. However, the one controlled study of 15 children, including 14 who had Separation Anxiety Disorder, failed to demonstrate a treatment effect (Allen, Leonard, & Swedo, 1995). Therefore, the use of benzodiazepines as a treatment in this disorder remains questionable.

Drug Treatment for Adults and Elderly with Pathologic Grief

One open trial of desipramine, and other of nortriptyline, as treatment for Major Depressive Episodes of bereavement in adults provide interesting observations on the effects of tricyclic treatment on separation anxiety. The first study reported on treatment response during a 4 week, open trial of desipramine (one case was treated with nortriptyline) among 10 persons ranging in age from 36 to 65 (Jacobs, Nelson, & Zisook, 1987). The participants were bereaved 12 months earlier and met SCID-DSM-III criteria for Major Depression. The average dosage of desipramine was 119 milligrams per day and ranged from 75 to 150 milligrams per day. At the end of 4 weeks, 7 of 10 persons had moderate to marked improvement of depressive symptoms on the Hamilton Depressive Rating Scale. In addition, 7 of 10 participants completed scores on separation anxiety before and after treatment. One person's score on separation anxiety was very low both before and after treatment. Three of the remaining six experienced reductions in intensity of separation anxiety of 50% or greater during the desipramine treatment. For the other 3, there was only a small effect.

A second study reported on treatment response to nortriptyline during a 16 week, open trial among 13 elderly persons (Pasternak et al., 1991). The subjects ranged in age from 61 to 78. They were bereaved on the average 11.9 months and met research diagnostic criteria for stable, Major Depression. The mean dose of nortriptyline at the time of response was 49.2 ± 13.5 mg/day with a mean steady state plasma level of 68.1 ± 19.4 ng/ml. At the end of 16 weeks, depressive symptoms were moderately to markedly improved in all 13 persons, with a decrease in Hamilton Depression Rating Scale scores of 67.9% from pretreatment (22.1 ± 3.6) to posttreatment (7.2 ± 2.8). The median response time was 6.4 weeks ($M = 9.6 \pm 82$). Scores on the Texas Revised Inventory of Grief, a measure of unresolved grief, were high before treatment ($M = 51.4$) and went down only 9.3%. Texas Revised Inventory of Grief scores did not reach the level of current (posttreatment) grief intensity reported by 20 nondepressed bereaved subjects ($M = 39.7$). Scores of the intensity of separation anxiety, measured by a different scale, declined approximately 50% from 16.2 ($SD = 7.6$) before treatment to 8.3 ($SD = 2.6$) after treatment. Note that this contrast between the two measures may prove that the measure of separation anxiety used in this study is a more sensitive measure of "state" separation anxiety, versus "trait separation anxiety", than the Texas Revised Inventory of Grief. Still, this study, along with the other of desipramine described above, raises a question of whether the response of separation anxiety to tricyclic antidepressants is less robust than the response of depressive symptoms.

In a study related conceptually to the open trials of fluoxetine in children with Separation Anxiety Disorder reviewed above, Zygmont and colleagues treated 15 persons with symptoms of Traumatic Grief in an open trial of paroxetine (Zygmont et al., 1998). In part the study was stimulated by the modest response of separation anxiety to tricyclics noted in the previous two studies. Average age of the sample was 57 years (range 40–79). Treatment began a median of 17 months (range 6–139) after a loss. In 4 cases, the loss was from death of a spouse, in 5, death of a child, and one each from death of a grandchild or parent. All the participants had scores on the Inventory of Complicated Grief (ICG) of 20 or greater, indicating caseness for Traumatic Grief. In addition, 10 persons met criteria for Major Depressive Disorder and most of the others had a diagnosis of Minor Depression, Depressed Disorder NOS, or Adjustment Disorder with Depressed Mood. The initial dose of paroxetine was 10 milligrams per day. The dose was increased weekly by 10 milligram increments to reach a maximum daily dose of 30 milligrams. If symptoms were not improved by the sixth week of treatment (a reduction in baseline ICG of less than 25%), the dose was increased to 40 milligrams. The severity of symptoms of Traumatic Grief diminished by 53% over 16 weeks. Depressive ratings on the Hamilton Depression Rating Scale improved by 54%. The change in depression scores correlated with change in traumatic grief scores (rho = .56, $p \leq .05$). GAS scores improved from 56.3 to 76.2. Of 21 persons who started treatment, 6 discontinued before completion of the protocol, 5 due to side effects and 1 through refusal of further treatment. Photosensitivity and impotence were the most common and troublesome side effects, but no other serious adverse effects were noted.

Stemming from the previous study, Zygmont and colleagues also reported a post hoc comparison of paroxetine and nortriptyline for symptoms of Traumatic Grief, using an archival contrast group (Zygmont et al., 1998). The paroxetine treated group was compared to 22 nortriptyline treated participants in a separate, ongoing, randomized, double blind, placebo controlled clinical trial for bereavement related major depressive episodes. Both pharmacologic treatments had an equally positive effect on the symptoms of Traumatic Grief and Major Depression over 16 weeks. The authors note that the paroxetine treated group was more diagnostically heterogeneous, had more persons with multiple diagnoses, and were bereaved more than twice as long as the nortriptyline group (16.6 versus 7.0 months). These differences conceivably rendered the paroxetine group more difficult to treat, making the post hoc comparison unfair. The authors noted a preference for selective serotonin reuptake inhibitors (SSRIs) in treatment of patients with symptoms of Traumatic Grief, given a low side effect profile, with fewer of the sedating, anticholinergic, or hypotensive effects of tricyclics, low lethality in overdose, and no need to monitor plasma levels, particularly among elderly patients.

Drug Treatment for Adults With Post-Traumatic Stress Disorder

Without entering into an extensive review of the literature, drug treatment studies of Post-Traumatic Stress Disorder (PTSD) suggest that selective serotonin reuptake inhibitors might be more effective for the broad range of symptoms of Traumatic Grief than tricyclic antidepressants. Tricyclics have a relatively selective effect on the intrusive, anxious, and depressive symptoms of PTSD (Davidson, Kudler, & Smith, 1990). Selective serotonin reuptake inhibitors have demonstrated a broader effect, including impact on the avoidant and numbing symptoms of PTSD in addition to the same symptom groups as tricyclics (Sutherland & Davidson, 1994).

Summary of the Drug Treatment Studies

In summary, this small review does not provide definitive evidence for reaching conclusions about psychotropic treatment of Traumatic Grief. The open trials of drug treatment must be followed up with randomized, controlled clinical studies of these agents. Also, the studies of childhood Separation Anxiety Disorder need to be repeated in adults with Traumatic Grief. Still, given the growing evidence of the effectiveness of selective serotonin reuptake inhibitors for separation anxiety and Separation Anxiety Disorder and their attractive side effects profiles, they appear to be leading candidates for further study. The idea that serotonin reuptake inhibitors might be more effective than tricyclics for symptoms of separation anxiety has not borne out in a small, open trial, however, it would be interesting to examine this issue in a randomized, controlled trial. Two randomized, controlled studies of selective serotonin reuptake inhibitors are already under way.

Choice of Medication, Dosage, and Duration of Treatment Given Current Knowledge

While we wait for more definitive evidence on drug treatment, experienced psychopharmacologists and experts in the field of bereavement are judiciously employing antidepressant treatments for disorders involving separation anxiety in children and adults. While preferences and leads in the field are summarized above, no definitive data at present indicates that a particular class of medications is more effective than another for the treatment of childhood Separation Anxiety Disorder or Traumatic

Grief. Therefore, for the time being, the choice of antidepressant, the dosage, and the duration of use in treating patients with symptoms of Traumatic Grief are clinical decisions that depend on the variables in each case and do not differ systematically from the decisions made in the general psychiatric clinic. In short, the selection of a medication should be based on past personal or family history of response to treatment in the circumstances of bereavement, if such history is available for the target symptoms of Traumatic Grief. In the absence of this information, side effect profiles, adverse effects, and toxicity guide the choice. Newer antidepressants agents such as selective serotonin reuptake inhibitors (and possibly buproprion or nefazodone) have the advantage of more tolerable side effects, which is particularly important in treating elderly patients. Furthermore, they are less lethal in overdose than the older tricyclics and monoamine oxidase inhibitors.

☐ Psychotherapy

A Study of Psychotherapy for Children and Adolescents with Separation Anxiety Disorder

There is only one study of psychotherapy in children and adolescents with Separation Anxiety Disorder that is salient in this review, again based on the assumption that Traumatic Grief is related to this disorder. Of note, Kendall reported a randomized, controlled, clinical trial of cognitive behavioral therapy (CBT) in 47 children with childhood anxiety disorders (Kendall, 1994). Ranging in age from 9 to 13, 8 of the children had a diagnosis of Separation Anxiety Disorder. Thirty-two percent of the sample had comorbid Major Depression. Seven doctoral students in clinical psychology provided the CBT for a period of 16 weeks in one-hour sessions. The therapy included two main components of 8 sessions each: education about cognitive and behavioral strategies for symptoms and exposure exercises using the newly learned cognitive and behavioral strategies. The therapy was individual and child focused, while maintaining numerous parent contacts. Participants were randomly assigned to treatment or a wait list condition. At the end of treatment, the children had significantly lower anxiety, depression, and general symptom scores, as well as reduced fears, improved coping, and improved behavior and social skills as rated by parents. Sixty percent of the treated cases were returned to nondeviant levels of symptoms. Post-treatment improvement and one year follow up assessments did not differ significantly, indicating the treatment effects were sustained. No adverse reactions were reported.

Studies of Psychotherapy in Adults with Pathologic Grief

Crisis Intervention

The literature contains three controlled studies of crisis intervention for acutely bereaved adults done during the 1970s. Two of these studies found positive results for the intervention (Raphael, 1977; Gerber, Wiener, Battin, & Arkin, 1975). One showed negative results (Polak, Egan, & Bandenbergh, 1975) and is reviewed in more detail elsewhere (Jacobs, 1993). In short, the latter study treated everyone regardless of diagnosis or risk and the therapy was minimally and loosely conceived, both of which may have contributed to the negative results.

One study by the psychiatrist Raphael is particularly notable (Raphael, 1977). She randomly assigned 31 high risk, acutely bereaved widows aged 60 or less to crisis intervention treatment and 33 to a control condition that received no intervention. Raphael provided the treatment that lasted three months in the weeks immediately after the loss. The intervention included support and review of positive and negative aspects of the lost relationship within the framework of psychodynamically oriented psychotherapy. For outcome assessment, the study used Goldberg's General Health Questionnaire, which measures somatic symptoms, depressive symptoms, anxiety, substance use, and work capacity. The treatment group had considerable reduction of symptom scores on the General Health Questionnaire by comparison with the controls at follow up 13 months after the loss.

Brief Dynamic Psychotherapy and other Therapies

Other studies have investigated specific therapies for pathologic or complicated grief. For example, Horowitz and colleagues (Horowitz, Marmar, Weiss, DeWitt, & Rosenbaum, 1984) treated 33 bereaved women and 2 bereaved men whose mean age was 31.4 years ($SD = 8.7$). The sample sought help on the average 6 months after the death of a parent. The treatment group received brief dynamic psychotherapy (BDP) from experienced clinicians. BDP included meeting once per week and lasted an average of 11.6 sessions. The treatment group was compared to a nonequivalent group of 37 field subjects who were not treated. Dynamic Psychotherapy focused on reviewing the relationship with the deceased, the death, individual core conflicts, and separation at the end of treatment. Both groups showed significant stress specific and general symptomatic relief over the course of study. No adverse reactions were reported. The treatment group started with a higher intensity of intrusive, avoidant, anxious, and depressive symptoms than the comparison group and declined faster towards the end of treatment. Approximately one year after the loss, the treatment group attained improved levels not significantly different from the field controls, with the exception of one domain of symptoms. The exception was avoidant symptoms which declined from high initial levels in the treatment group but ended the year at about the same initial level of the comparison group, who had declined significantly to even lower levels. Still, the authors note that the major difference between the two groups over time was a decline in the patients' avoidance of themes and emotions evoked by the death.

In a related study, Marmar and colleagues randomly assigned 31 women, who sought treatment 4 months to 3 years after a loss, to brief dynamic psychotherapy (Marmar, Horowitz, Weiss, Wilner, & Kaltreider (1988). Thirty controls were assigned to mutual help group treatment led by nonclinicians. Experienced clinicians provided brief dynamic psychotherapy that lasted 12 sessions and is described above. Ten women dropped out of psychotherapy and 23 women were dropped out of the mutual help groups. Both groups experienced reductions in stress specific and general symptoms as well as improvement in social and work functioning. The symptomatic improvement emerged as a statistical trend at the completion of treatment (12 weeks) and became significant at the time of a 4 month follow up after treatment.

There are no reported controlled trials of interpersonal therapy (IPT) or cognitive behavioral therapy (CBT) specifically for bereaved adults with pathologic grief. Of historical note, it is worth recalling that one of the case studies in the manual for IPT was a bereaved, depressed woman (Klerman, Weissman, Rounsaville, & Chevron, 1984). In one, open, noncontrolled, nonrandomized trial of IPT, Miller and colleagues reported treatment for three male and three female elderly patients (mean age = 68) with bereavement related depression (Miller et al., 1994). The patients entered treatment 11–56 (mean = 26) weeks after the death of their spouse. The IPT lasted 17 sessions. IPT reduced depression scores after treatment on the 17 item Hamilton Depression Rating Scale from 18.5 ($\pm$ 2.3) to 7.2 ($\pm$ 4.6). In addition, a more modest reduction in scores on the Texas Revised Inventory of Grief from 49.3 ($\pm$ 9.6) to 39.2 ($\pm$ 14.9) was noted over the course of treatment.

Behavior Therapies

Several reports of brief, behavior therapy for pathologic grief appear in literature. Most of them, while reporting benefit from the behavioral treatment, are small and uncontrolled (Gauthier & Pye, 1979; Hodgkinson, 1982; Lieberman, 1978). They focus on exposure and habituation to feared and avoided bereavement cues as the primary strategy within the framework of a phobic model of pathologic grief (Kavanagh, 1990). In the first controlled clinical trial of behavior therapy, Mawson and colleagues provided behavior therapy (guided mourning) for bereaved adults (11 women, 1 man; age range 28–61) with chronic grief of at least one year's duration (Mawson, Marks, Ramm, & Stern, 1981). Half of 12 persons were randomized to guided mourning three times a week for two weeks, where the patient was exposed to painful and avoided reminders of the loss. The other half were assigned to a control treatment where they were encouraged to avoid such reminders. Those receiving the guided mourning treatment improved significantly more than the controls on phobic symptoms, phobic distress, and the Texas Inventory of Grief. The effects of treatment on depressive symptom scores was less evident than the effect on specific measures of grief and phobic avoidance behavior.

Sireling and colleagues replicated this first controlled clinical study of guided mourning in a randomized, controlled trial of 26 adults with morbid grief (Sireling, Cohen, & Marks, 1988). They compare guided mourning with a control treatment in which bereaved persons were instructed to avoid painful and feared bereavement cues. The treated group had a significant reduction in cue avoidance, avoidance distress, and somatic symptoms by comparison with the anti-exposure group. The improvement was sustained for up to 9 months of follow up. Both the guided mourning group and controls improved on the Texas Inventory of Grief, anxiety, depressive symptoms, work functioning, and social functioning. The pattern of response to this behavioral treatment (exposure) suggested that there might be partial independence of bereavement avoidance from both depressive symptoms and preoccupation with the deceased (a hallmark of separation anxiety).

Kleber and Brom compared three therapies: trauma desensitization (a behavioral therapy including exposure and relaxation techniques), hypnosis (based on learning theory), and a brief, dynamic psychodynamic psychotherapy (based on Horowitz), in a Dutch study of 83 bereaved adults with pathologic grief from losses in the previous 5 years (Kleber & Brom, 1987). There were 60 women and 23 men, and the average age of the group was 42 (range 18–73). In addition, there was a group of 18 matched controls referred to a waiting list. It is unclear if the participants were randomly assigned to treatment or not. Treatment occurred on average 23 months after the loss and lasted 15–20 sessions. Many of the losses were unexpected or frankly traumatic, causing considerable traumatic symptoms in the sample. All the treatments combined were significantly more effective than the control situation. This was true for symptoms of intrusion, avoidance, anxiety, and somatic symptoms, and the improvement was sustained during an unspecified period of follow up. In residual gain analyses of the individual therapies, the authors observed significant change only for the symptoms of intrusion and avoidance. In these analyses, trauma desensitization had the biggest effect followed by lesser, but significant effects for hypnosis and psychodynamic therapy. Psychodynamic therapy was effective for anxious and avoidant symptoms but not intrusive symptoms. Younger patients and those with internal locus of control had better outcomes from all the therapies. Also, low income patients benefited more from behavior treatment and less from psychodynamic therapy. The reverse was true for high income persons. Strong feelings of anger were negatively related to outcome except in the case of hypnotherapy.

Summary of Psychotherapy Studies

As we found in the case of psychopharmacologic treatment there is a need for more controlled, clinical trials of psychotherapy for Traumatic Grief. In this review of existing studies on Separation Anxiety Disorder in children or pathologic grief in adults, both psychodynamically oriented treatments and behavioral/cognitive treatments have some proven effectiveness and hold promise for Traumatic Grief. The potential of these two quite different types of psychotherapy highlight an argument for some of the nonspecific elements of therapy discussed in Raphael's recent review (Raphael, Middleton, Martinek, & Misso, 1993). These include a genuine, empathic, and compassionate relationship to the therapist and a knowledge of loss and grief that the therapist imparts to the patient (Raphael, Middleton, Martinek, & Misso, 1993). Reviewing the relationship to the deceased person and the circumstances of the death also emerge as common foci of therapy in the review above.

The potential of two quite different types of therapy to help also raises the possibility of different therapies for different people with different problems and different domains of symptoms. There is much to learn about what in a therapy works on what aspect of the disorder and for whom. For example, Kendall and colleagues, in CBT treatment of children with Separation Anxiety Disorder raise a question of whether it is the educational or the behavioral parts of CBT that are effective (Kendall, 1994).

In another vein, two different study groups with two different therapies for adults find a prominent effect of therapy on avoidance of feared or painful reminders of the death (Mawson et al., 1981; Horowitz et al., 1984). These latter observations raise questions about whether avoidant symptoms are core target symptoms for any therapy as well as questions about what therapies might address other aspects of the problem (Kavanagh, 1990).

There is much ferment in the field of development of psychotherapies for Traumatic Grief. This is reflected in a recent volume on psychotherapy that integrates knowledge from thanatology (studies of loss) and trauma (Rando, 1993). The interest in psychotherapies for Traumatic Grief is also reflected in a recent issue of *In Session: Psychotherapy in Practice* (Rynearson, 1996; Worden, 1996; Zisook and Shuchter, 1996). For instance, Rynearson is formulating guidelines for an innovative therapy for survivors of violent deaths (Rynearson, 1996). Worden's task oriented approach to psychotherapy of the clinical complications of bereavement is time honored and updated in this journal. Also, Zisook and colleagues have proposed guidelines for a biologically informed approach to psychotherapy of depressions of bereavement providing a far reaching reconceptualization of the emphasis in psychotherapy (Zisook & Shuchter, 1996; Shuchter, Downs, & Zisook, 1996). Finally, Frank and colleagues recently described the development of a cognitive behavioral treatment for Traumatic Grief, based on Foa's treatment for PTSD (Shear & Frank, 1998). These innovations offer the hope of considerable progress in development of psychotherapies for Traumatic Grief over the next few years.

Self-help Groups

Without entering into an extensive review of evaluative studies of self-help groups, it is important to mention their potential contribution to an overall treatment plan. There is a wide variety of self-help groups with several features: a membership that shares a common experience, self governance, a value of self-reliance, and accessibility without charge (Lieberman, 1993). Generally speaking, self-help groups can supplement treatment by offering the inculcation of hope, the development of understanding, social supports, a source of normalization or universalization, and a setting to learn and practice new coping skills.

Data on self-help groups are hard to collect given the groups' nature as open, voluntary organizations that are often skeptical of professionals. There is insufficient data to address questions about the efficacy and efficiency of self-help intervention, what types of bereavement might benefit, and when to provide self-help intervention in the course of bereavement (Lieberman, 1993). Still, many bereaved persons become involved in them, and one study, reviewed above by Marmor and colleagues, suggests they are just as effective as brief, dynamic psychotherapy when the self-help groups have leaders screened for suitability by professionals and trained using a manual on conducting self-help group interventions (Marmar et al., 1988).

☐ Conclusion

I argue that Traumatic Grief is a true, new diagnostic entity that we should incorporate into clinical practice. A corollary is that the diagnosis of Traumatic Grief justifies treatment. Careful differential diagnosis is necessary first. Based on the literature and my own experience, I believe the risks of both psychopharmacologic and psychotherapeutic treatments are small. While there is growing evidence of the efficacy of both psychotropic and psychotherapeutic treatments, proven efficacy remains a central and pressing question. Undoubtedly, there is a need for controlled clinical trials to scientifically establish the benefit of treatment (or not). Still, given the existing evidence and despite its limitations, I advocate more active consideration of treatment for Traumatic Grief. Whatever treatments are selected, when bereaved persons seek help during acute bereavement, treatment ought to occur based on individualized treatment plans in an integrated framework of care that incorporates knowledge of the natural process of grief. The next chapter discusses a diagnosis/treatment algorithm that helps to apply the ideas of diagnosis and treatment developed in chapters 3, 4, and here in a more individualized way.

☐ References

Allen, A. J., Leonard, H., & Swedo, S. E. (1995). Current knowledge of medications for the treatment of childhood anxiety disorders. *Journal of the American Academy of Child and Adolescent Psychiatry, 34,* 976–986.

Bernstein, G. A., Garfinkel, B. D., & Borchardt, C. M. (1990). Comparative studies of pharmacotherapy for school refusal. *Journal of the American Academy of Child and Adolescent Psychiatry, 29,* 773–781.

Birmaher, B., Waterman, G. S., Ryan, N., Cully, M., Balach, L., Ingram, J., & Brodsky, M. (1994). Fluoxetine for childhood anxiety disorders. *Journal of the American Academy of Child and Adolescent Psychiatry, 33,* 933–999.

Davidson, J., Kudler, H., & Smith, R. (1990). Treatment of post-traumatic stress disorder with amytriptyline and placebo. *Archives of General Psychiatry, 47,* 259–266.

Engel, G. L. (1961). Is grief a disease? A challenge for medical research. *Psychosomatic Medicine, 23,* 18–22.

Fairbanks, J. M., Pine, D. S., Tancer, N. K., Dummit, E. S. III, Kentgen, L. M., Martin, J., Asche, B. K., & Klein, R. G. (1997). Open fluoxetine treatment of mixed anxiety disorders in children and adolescents. *Journal of Child and Adolescent Psychopharmacology, 7,* 17–29.

Gerber, I., Wiener, A., Battin, D., & Arkin, A. M. (1975). Brief therapy to the aged bereaved. In B. Shoenberg, I. Gerber, (Eds.), *Bereavement: Its psychosocial aspect.* New York: Columbia University Press.

Gittelman, R., Klein, D. F. (1971). Controlled imipramine treatment of school children. *Archives of General Psychiatry, 25,* 204–411.

Gauthier, J., Pye, C. (1979). Graduated self-exposure in management of grief. *Behavioral Analysis and Modification, 3,* 202–208.

Hodgkinson, P. E. (1982). Abnormal grief—the problem of therapy. *British Journal of Medical Psychology, 55,* 29–34.

Horowitz, M. J., Marmar, C., Weiss, D. S., De Witt, K. N., & Rosenbaum, R. (1984). Brief psychotherapy of bereavement reactions: The relationship of process to outcome. *Archives of General Psychiatry, 41,* 438–448.

Jacobs, S. C., Nelson, J. C., & Zisook, S. (1987). Treating depressions of bereavement with antidepressants: A pilot study. *Psychiatric Clinics of North America, 10,* 501–510.

Jacobs, S. (1993). *Pathologic grief: Maladaptation to loss.* Washington, DC: American Psychiatric Press.

Kavanagh, D. J. (1990). Towards a cognitive-behavioural intervention for adult grief reactions. *British Journal of Psychiatry, 157,* 373–383.

Kendall, P. C. (1994). Treating anxiety disorders in children: Results of a randomized clinical trial. *Journal of Consulting and Clinical Psychology, 62,* 100–110.

Kleber, R. J., & Brom, D. (1987). Psychotherapy and pathological grief: Controlled outcome study. *Israeli Journal of Psychiatry and Related Sciences, 24,* 99–109.

Klein, R. G., Koplewitz, H. S., & Kanner, A. (1992). Imipramine treatment of children with separation anxiety disorder. *Journal of the American Academy of Child and Adolescent Psychiatry, 31,* 21–28.

Klerman, G. L., Weissman, M. M., Rounsaville, B. J., & Chevron, E. S. (1984). *Interpersonal psychotherapy of depression.* New York: Basic Books.

Lieberman, M. A. (1993). Bereavement self-help groups: A review of conceptual and methodological issues. In M. S. Stroebe, W. Stroebe, R. O. Hansson, (Eds.), *Handbook of bereavement: Theory, research, and intervention* (pp. 411–426). Cambridge, England: Cambridge University Press.

Lieberman, S. (1978). Nineteen cases of morbid grief. *British Journal of Psychiatry, 132,* 159–163.

Marmar, C. R., Horowitz, M. J., Weiss, D. S., Wilner, N. R., & Kaltreider, N. B. (1988). A controlled trial of brief psychotherapy and mutual help group treatment of conjugal bereavement. *American Journal of Psychiatry, 145,* 203–209.

Mawson, D., Marks, I. M., Ramm, L., & Stern, R. S. (1981). Guided mourning for morbid grief: A controlled study. *British Journal of Psychiatry, 138,* 185–193.

Miller, M. D., Frank, E., Cornes, C., Imber, S., Anderson, B., Ehrenpreis, L., Malloy, J., Silberman, R., Wolfson, L., Zaltman, J., & Reynolds, C. F. (1994). Applying interpersonal psychotherapy to bereavement-related depression following loss of a spouse in late life. *Journal of Psychotherapy Practice and Research, 3,* 149–162.

Pasternak, R. E., Reynolds, C. F., Schlernitzauer, M., Hoch, C. C., Buysse, D. J., Houck, P. R., Perel, J. M. (1991). Acute open-trial nortriptyline therapy of bereavement-related depression in late life. *Journal of Clinical Psychiatry, 52,* 307–310.

Polak, P. B., Egan, D., & Bandenbergh, R. (1975). Prevention in mental health: A controlled study. *American Journal of Psychiatry, 132,* 146–149.

Rando, T. A. (1993). *Treatment of complicated mourning.* Champaign, Ill: Research Press.

Raphael, B. (1977). Preventive intervention with the recently bereaved. *Archives of General Psychiatry, 34,* 1450–1454.

Raphael, B., Middleton, W., Martinek, N., & Misso, V. (1993). Counseling and therapy of the bereaved. In M. S. Stroebe, W. Stroebe, & R. O. Hansson, (Eds.), *Handbook of*

Bereavement: Theory, research, and intervention. (pp. 427–453. Cambridge, England: Cambridge University Press.

Rynearson, E. K., (1996). Psychotherapy of bereavement after homicide: Be offensive. *In Session: Psychotherapy in Practice, 2,* 47–57.

Shear, K., & Frank, E. (1998). Cognitive behavior treatment for traumatic grief (Abs.). Presented at the Society for Psychotherapy Research, Snowbird, UT, June 24–27.

Shuchter, S. R., Downs, N., & Zisook, S. (1996). *Biologically informed psychotherapy for depression.* New York: Guilford Publications.

Sireling, L., Cohen, D., & Marks, I. (1988). Guided mourning for morbid grief: A replication. *Behavior Therapy, 19,* 121–132.

Sutherland, S., & Davidson, J. (1994). Pharmacotherapy for post-traumatic stress disorder. *Psychiat Clinics of N America, 17,* 409–423.

Worden, J. W. (1996). Tasks and mediators of mourning: A guideline for the mental health practitioner. *In Session: Psychotherapy in Practice, 2,* 73–80.

Zisook, S., Shuchter, S. R. (1996). Psychotherapy of the depressions in spousal bereavement. *In Session: Psychotherapy in Practice, 2,* 31–45.

Zygmont, M., Prigerson, H. G., Houck, P. R., Miller, M. D., Shear, M. K., Jacobs, S. C., & Reynolds, C. F. (1998). A post-hoc comparison of paroxetine and nortriptyline for symptoms of traumatic grief. *Journal of Clinical Psychiatry, 59,* 241–255.

A Diagnosis/Treatment Algorithm for Traumatic Grief

The practicing clinician is faced with the challenge of how to integrate psychopharmacologic treatment, psychotherapy, and self-help group interventions into a coherent, multimodal, individualized treatment plan for each patient with Traumatic Grief. Optimally, the treatment is also set at the appropriate level of intensity for the severity and risk of the disorder in each case. The following is a discussion of a diagnosis/treatment algorithm for Traumatic Grief that I have developed over the past 25 years. It is a personal approach that stems from chapters 3, 4, and 5 and also goes beyond them by refining somewhat and supplementing the ideas on diagnosis and treatment. The algorithm is based on data from systematic studies when it is available. Given the limitations of available data, it also draws on several years of personal, clinical experience in evaluating and treating patients with clinical complications of bereavement. It is illustrated in part by using the case examples that have already been introduced in previous chapters.

☐ A Diagnosis/Treatment Algorithm for Traumatic Grief

A diagnosis/treatment algorithm for Traumatic Grief follows 4 steps (see Table 1). The algorithm is based on the assumption that a patient has

TABLE 1   Diagnosis/Treatment Algorithm

Evaluative step	Finding	Treatment
1. Severity of symptoms		
A) Signal symptoms of suicidal ideation fear losing control funct. impairment	Present	Intensive, multimodal
	Absent	Conservative, single mode
B) ICG score	High	Intensive, multimodal
	Low	Conservative, single mode
Go to next step		
2. Timing and duration of syndrome		
	Early, short	Monitoring, conservative, single mode, probably psychotherapy first
	Late, short, or long	Intensive, multimodal
Go to next step		
3. Risk factors		
	Low load	Conservative, single mode
	High load	Intensive, multimodal
Go to next step		
4. Comorbidity		
PTSD	Present	Emphasize PTSD, intensive, multimodal
MDE	Present	Monitor both syndromes, intensive, multimodal
Panic disorder	Present	Same as MDE
No comorbidity	Absent	Target symptoms of Traumatic Grief

presented during bereavement and meets criteria for Traumatic Grief. The algorithm includes the evaluation of four aspects of the symptoms of such patients: 1) the severity of the symptoms reflected in 3 signal symptoms and a symptom score for Traumatic Grief, 2) the timing and duration of the Traumatic Grief during bereavement, 3) the loading of risk factors for Traumatic Grief, and 4) the presence of comorbidity such as Post-traumatic Stress Disorder, Major Depression, or Panic Disorder.

When the indicators in the algorithm are positive and when they accumulate, the treatment plan ought to be intensive—meeting at least once weekly, if not more often—multimodal—including psychotropic treatment, psychotherapy, and sometimes mutual support groups—and implemented immediately. When the indicators are absent and the risk is low, the pace of the treatment plan can be more discretionary, conservative, of a single mode, and implemented in progressive stages.

To begin the algorithm, I note if three signal symptoms are present as part of the Traumatic Grief syndrome. A signal symptom simply means a symptom that serves as a red flag when encountered during an evaluation. Signal symptoms are suicidal ideation, fear of losing control, and marked functional impairment and generally connote the severity of the disorder, while having specific implications for intervention.

The importance of suicidal ideation has face validity that requires little further explanation. There is a higher risk of suicide among bereaved persons (see chapter 4), and there is some evidence that it is higher among those with symptoms of Traumatic Grief and among late life widowers. When suicidal ideation is present, the clinician must evaluate the risk. Both Mrs. C. and Mr. D. (chapter 4) reported suicidal ideation, however, I evaluated their risk as low. If the risk is high and imminent, the treatment plan ought to be intensive, multimodal, and implemented immediately.

Another signal symptom is fear of losing control. This symptom is often an index of the intensity of subjective distress, the severity of the syndrome, and to some extent, the presence of an obsessive personality style. It is often associated with severe anxiety (panic attacks) or a depressive syndrome (Clayton, Halikas, & Maurice, 1971). Both Mrs. A. (chapter 1), who developed a depressive syndrome and had an obsessive personality style, and Mrs. B. (chapter 3), whose symptoms crescendoed in intensity and who eventually developed a depressive syndrome and had several panic attacks, reported this symptom. When present, particularly in the circumstances of suicidal ruminations or hostile impulses, it signals a level of severity that justifies more intensive, multimodal treatment, unless the patient responds immediately and affirmatively to reassurance and the offer to help.

The last signal symptom is marked impairment in psychosocial functioning. This symptom is an index of severity in the sense that the symptomatic disturbance is linked to impairment in functioning. When present, the clinician must evaluate the patient's risk of losing a job or damaging important relationships to family or intimates. This problem was probably most pressing for Mrs. A. who was most notably impaired in psychosocial functioning. Mrs. B. was probably the least impaired, but all of the case examples reported at least middling functional impairment. When the risk of serious consequences of the illness are high, the stakes of treatment are augmented. This justifies a more intensive, multimodal treatment plan.

The availability of the ICG in the past few years has strengthened the first step in this algorithm (Prigerson et al., 1995). The use of these signal symptoms can be couched now in an ICG score which serves as a guide to the intensity of the symptoms. When the score is high, there is a need for intensive, multimodal treatment. All of the patients used as case examples in this text, with the exception of Mrs. B., whose symptoms evolved over time and built in intensity, presented symptoms of high intensity on first meeting.

The second step for deciding on a treatment plan, after looking for signal symptoms depends on the timing and duration of the Traumatic Grief syndrome. When a diagnosis is made in the first few months after the death, the duration of the syndrome is only one month or so, and when the syndrome does not include the signal symptoms (i.e., the intensity is low), the treatment plan can be more conservative. The absence of risk factors for Traumatic Grief, or their minimal practice, reinforces a conservative approach to treatment. For example, in mildly to moderately severe cases without a high loading of risk factors or comorbidity, therapy might be initiated without the use of antidepressant or anti-anxiety drugs, reserving them for use later, if there is no response to the therapy or if the symptoms intensify. On the other hand, when the diagnosis is made later in the course of bereavement, the syndrome is well established, and signal symptoms are present, vigorous, multimodal treatment is indicated.

The third step in this diagnosis/treatment algorithm is the evaluation of risk factors for Traumatic Grief. The risk factors include a violent death of the deceased, young age, female gender, loss of a spouse or child, a problematic relationship to the deceased person, dependent or schizoid personality traits, or an inability to come to terms with the death during a terminal illness. For a more thorough review of risk factors for Traumatic Grief, see chapter 7. If a patient presents for evaluation early in the course of bereavement (first 4 to 6 months after the death), the presence or absence of risk factors helps in making judgments about the potential course of the syndrome. If risk factors are highly loaded for a particular patient, the syndrome tends to be more severe and there is a greater probability of a prolonged course of the syndrome. If multiple risk factors are present, they tip the scale towards more vigorous, multimodal treatment. For example, Mr. D. probably had the greatest loading of risk factors, including the violent death of his daughter. The sudden, untimely nature of the death made it impossible for him to take leave of his daughter. It is also notable that he presented late in the course of illness. This and other considerations militated for aggressive treatment. Mrs. A. was a close second for presence of risk factors. In her case, they included bereavement overload, the untimely death of her son, and her gender. The evaluation of risk factors was probably most useful for Mrs. B. She presented early in the course of bereavement with moderately intense symptoms. Her loading of risk factors, including the sudden, unexpected, somewhat traumatic death of her husband, clinging attachment style, problematic relationship to her husband, and early losses, was high. Her case illustrates how the evaluation of risk factors for Traumatic Grief is a strategy that is useful principally in the early stages of the course of the disorder.

The fourth step involves evaluation of comorbidity. If a coexisting Posttraumatic Stress Disorder (PTSD) is present, it is conventional wisdom at present (Rando, 1993; Rynearson, 1996; Raphael, Middleton, Martinek, & Misso, 1993; Pynoos & Nader, 1993), that primary emphasis in psychotherapy, if not the whole treatment plan, ought to be on the symptoms of PTSD. As I have noted before this assumption requires systematic testing. In the treatment of patients with comorbid PTSD and Traumatic Grief, Rando urges the integration of knowledge from studies of thanatology and studies of trauma, fields, that are often isolated from each other (Rando, 1993). Rynearson emphasizes that the treatment should focus on three things: the traumatizing aspects of the death, avoidance, and desensitization from feared stimuli (Rynearson, 1996). Comorbidity of PTSD also places emphasis on the choice of a selective serotonin reuptake inhibitor, if a drug is used. While emphasizing the treatment of the symptoms of PTSD, symptoms of Traumatic Grief need not, and should not, be ignored. Still, based on current, conventional wisdom, to the extent that a treatment strategy for Traumatic Grief differs or conflicts with treatment for PTSD, the treatment of the PTSD would take precedence early in the course of treatment. Also, the existence of comorbidity argues for more intensive, multimodal treatment.

If there is a coexisting Major Depressive Episode, the main implication for clinicians is the need to monitor two domains of symptoms. In other words, the clinician must monitor both the depressive symptoms and the symptoms of Traumatic Grief, even though the treatment might be quite similar for both. As in the case of coexisting PTSD, the treatment ought to be more intensive and multimodal, including treatment for both types of symptoms. Sometimes, there is a counterpoint between these two separate domains of symptoms, with one group of symptoms waxing while the other wanes. For example, a patient's depressive symptoms may be responding nicely to antidepressant treatment (in my experience, usually with tricyclic antidepressants), but the patient comes in for the next session fearing a relapse. In this situation, it important to clearly identify the nature of the symptoms. If the symptoms are depressive, the first thoughts as a reaction to a depressive relapse or nonresponse would be considering the adequacy of the length of the drug trial, augmenting the dose, and thinking about switching the antidepressant. If the symptoms reflect separation distress, the clinical strategy includes educating the patient about the nature of the symptoms, monitoring the symptoms, and then considering a change in the dose or antidepressant. Even if the clinical process eventually leads to the same treatment decision, at least it is based on a more precise analysis.

The implications of coexisting Panic Disorder involve monitoring those symptoms as well as those of Traumatic Grief, as in the case of a comorbid Major Depression Episode. If antidepressants are used for treating the Traumatic Grief, the initial dosage might be lower and dosage increments more gradual to avoid pharmacologic aggravation of panic attacks. For example, although Mrs. B. did not meet criteria for Panic Disorder, she did report several panic attacks with the second series of attacks occurring at the initiation of antidepressant treatment during her second period of treatment.

☐ Personal Notes on Psychotherapy and Psychotropic Drugs

Having reviewed the evidence for treatments for Traumatic Grief in chapter 5 and found the evidence in an early stage of development, here I make a few personal notes on treatment while the field awaits additional studies.

I suggest an approach to psychotherapy of Traumatic Grief called brief, integrated, problem focused psychotherapy (Jacobs, 1993; Jacobs & Prigerson, 1996). It is a common sense approach to psychotherapy for experienced therapists and depends on the specific problems and needs of each patient. It emphasizes an empathic clinical relationship and psychoeducation. An empathic clinical relationship serves as an infrastructure for expert education about the nature of death, loss, normal bereavement, traumatic circumstances, Traumatic Grief, and other clinical complications of bereavement. An empathic doctor/patient relationship is also a platform that can be used for patient encouragement when urging him or her to surmount avoidance of feared aspects of the loss. In this sense, my approach to psychotherapy integrates the building blocks of both psychodynamic and cognitive, behavioral therapies.

Also, in a flexible approach to therapy, I suggest that the therapist ought to incorporate elements of different, specific, therapeutic strategies into treatment depending on the patient's problems. For example, techniques of interpersonal psychotherapy (IPT), designed to clarify interpersonal relationships and roles, are useful for unresolved conflicts with the deceased person or role transitions (Klerman, Weissman, Rounsaville, & Chevron, 1984). Attention to this helps the survivor remember and maintain an ongoing, adaptive relationship to the deceased person (Rando, 1993; Jacobs, 1993; Shuchter, Downs, & Zisook, 1996; Klass, 1996). Techniques of cognitive-behavioral therapy (CBT) are useful for monitoring and curbing depressive (i.e., pessimistic and helpless) or anxiogenic (i.e., fearful and weak) cognitive schemas (Beck, Rush, Shaw, & Emery, 1979). They can also be applied for reality testing of survival guilt and rage at persons perceived as not having prevented the death. The psychodynamic and interpretive techniques of brief dynamic psychotherapy (BDP) are useful for addressing identification symptoms, maladaptive attachment styles, low functioning personality traits, and latent self-images, including fears of abandonment (Horowitz et al., 1984). Finally, modern therapy should be biologically informed (Zisook & Shuchter, 1996; Shuchter et al., 1996). For example, manifestations of a disorder, such as a disturbance of self-esteem during a Major Depressive Episode, are understood as symptoms and not interpreted as causes of the illness.

Psychotherapy should be based on knowledge of and support for the normal processes of grief and the individual's active efforts to cope and adapt to his or her new circumstances. This assertion is just saying in specific terms for the psychotherapy of Traumatic Grief what should be true of any therapy. The total clinical picture of Traumatic Grief includes the efforts of the bereaved person to cope with the problems and feelings caused by the death of a significant other (Jacobs, Kasl, Schaefer, & Ostfeld, 1994). In discussing diagnosis in chapter 3, I said that coping phenomena are secondary in making a descriptive diagnosis when using the consensus criteria. On the other hand, sensitivity to a person's coping style can be instrumental in assuring adherence to treatment. A person's coping processes include both conscious cognitions and behaviors for the purpose of managing stressful demands and unconscious ego defenses for the purpose of maintaining psychological homeostasis (Jacobs, 1993, chapter 7). Both types can be adaptive or maladaptive in coping with a loss. Adaptive coping is an essential component of the process of spontaneous recovery from the death of an intimate. Alert clinicians need to know about coping processes and foster the healthier ones. It is important to avoid simple assumptions such as the idea that the nature of bereavement requires mainly, or even exclusively, emotion focused coping, no matter how important this may be at the outset of bereavement. An analysis of the tasks, new roles, and demands for new skills facing bereaved persons includes many challenges that require problem focused coping (Jacobs, 1993). Indeed, empirical analyses have found that problem focused coping predicts good outcome (Jacobs, Kasl, Schaefer, Ostfeld, 1994). Thus, both emotion focused and problem focused coping is needed in a flexible approach to coping with a loss. As a general proposition, I would say that bereavement requires different types of coping at different stages of the process for the differing problems an individual confronts. In other words, flexible and complex coping patterns are optimal for recovery. I believe that well chosen mutual support groups, particularly late in the first year of bereavement or during the second year or later, offer an excellent laboratory for the bereaved person to learn and practice effective, and sometimes new, coping skills.

In my experience, mutual support interventions are seldom indicated or effective early in the course of bereavement and can be counter productive. Early bereavement is a time when most bereaved persons turn to and rely on family and intimates. Mutual support interventions sometimes are indicated from 6 to 12 months after a death, and they become more salient and useful after the first year of bereavement, when, on average, the intensity of the subjective distress has subsided adequately. At the right time, mutual support interventions provide an important component of treatment.

In practice, I rarely use antidepressant medicine until 4 months of bereavement have elapsed, unless key indicators or multiple indicators of symptom severity, impairment, and risk are present. For many years I used desipramine or nortriptyline largely because of their effectiveness and advantageous side effect profiles. Recently, I have routinely used serotonin reuptake inhibitors because of their even more advantageous side effect profile and on the hypothesis that they may have greater efficacy. The occasion to use other, newer antidepressants has not come up in my practice, nor have augmentation strategies for refractory, depressive symptoms.

When Traumatic Grief is severe, prolonged, and disabling, multimodal treatment including drugs, psychotherapy, and mutual support is usually necessary. In addition, there is frequently a need to coordinate treatment with a family physician whom the patient has consulted for physical symptoms. For these reasons, an interdisciplinary team approach is often called for in treatment. For interdisciplinary treatment to be optimal it is important that all the elements of treatment be integrated into a comprehensive treatment plan. Also the treatment team members must communicate, if not meet, regularly to coordinate the various modes of treatment and discuss ongoing evaluation of the clinical picture as it evolves. Each professional person brings special skills, such as medical treatments for the psychiatrist or family interventions for the social worker, as well as generic skills, such as psychotherapy, to the task of treatment. When team members know each other through regularly working together, there is a clear assignment of responsibilities under a team leader, and when excellent communication is achieved, interdisciplinary treatment is more likely to succeed.

☐ Clinical Narrative

The substrate of the clinical processes of evaluation and treatment is the patient's story of the death and its consequences for his or her life. Tucker emphasizes the need for narrative in the development of diagnosis (Tucker, 1988) not to mention the creation of a context for treatment. In the absence of narrative, a diagnosis is a hollow set of criteria that ignores the unique person who is ill. In the absence of narrative and the context it creates, decisions about treatment run the risk of becoming crude and mechanical. The story of the patient, as it evolves in therapy, is an important product of therapy. Diagnosis and treatment are optimal not only when a clinician appreciates the diagnosis and knows about treatment, but also through the development of narrative. In other words, the clinician must attend to the person who is ill.

Narrative is nowhere most important than in the diagnosis and treatment of stress related disorders and, in particular, Traumatic Grief. The diagnosis can only be made when the context is right, that is, in the circumstances of the death of a significant other. An appreciation of risk factors, which lend each case its unique character, comes naturally from the clinician's commitment to elicit a narrative from a patient. Once the diagnosis is made, narrative is essential for treatment, too. One of the key tasks of psychotherapy is a review in detail of the events of the death in order to clarify traumatic elements and plan desensitization strategies. Narrative also supports a review of the relationship to the deceased person, which also figures largely as a task in therapy. Finally, a carefully developed narrative will provide a better understanding of the interplay of comorbid disorders, if they exist, with Traumatic Grief. For these reasons, the development of narrative is essential for the diagnosis and treatment of Traumatic Grief.

On another level, the development of narrative lends itself to a humanistic appreciation and commitment to each individual who is ill. This creates a foundation for caring for the patient, and as Peabody once reminded us in his time honored dictum, "the secret of the care of the patient is in caring for the patient" (Peabody, 1977).

☐ More Notes on Treatment From the Case Examples

As partly noted above, the four cases presented in previous chapter illustrate many of the points of discussion. I have pointed out where each of the cases fit best into the algorithm in terms of signal symptoms, timing and duration of the syndrome, risk factors assessment, and occurrence of comorbidity. I will amplify some notes on their treatment here.

All of the treatments required a sound clinician patient relationship that was employed to provide sympathetic encouragement to confront and understand feared aspects of the deaths and avoidance of them. Education about the person's experience of separation distress and traumatic distress was a platform for most of what I undertook in treatment for each of the patients. In each case, review of the facts of the death and the relationship to the deceased person was instrumental in elucidating the problems and fears latent in coping with the symptoms.

Specifically for Mrs. A., the bereaved mother in chapter 1, education, monitoring of maladaptive anxious and depressive cognitive schemata, interpretations of the identification symptoms, and review of her relationships to her mother and children were particularly important. Her avoidance was tied up with fears of irrationality, if not insanity, and I needed to address this through education about grief while encouraging her to confront some of the feared aspects of her experience. She had well entrenched depressive, and some anxious, cognitive schemata that I identified and encouraged her to monitor. Interpretation of her concerns about a personality change after the death of her son and mother, both as a reflection of the trauma and as an identification symptom, provided her a way of understanding that she found useful. Through such learning experiences, she seemed to become eager for a new understanding of her bereavement experience, which supported her characteristic, active style of coping. In this way, development of the story of her losses was a notable infrastructure of the treatment for this woman. Review of her relationships to her mother and children was another key part of her treatment. She refused to take antidepressant medicine as she wanted to surmount the symptoms without drugs. In this case, although I recommended multimodal treatment, I was obligated to focus on psychotherapy supplemented by a mutual support group that I had helped organize and train at the hospice where her mother died. The mutual support group supported her seeking treatment and thereby provided an additional buttress in this skeptical and avoidant, bereaved mother. Her psychotherapy is described in more detail as a case example in an article where I outline my personal approach to psychotherapy (Jacobs & Prigerson, 1996).

In contrast to Mrs. A., my approach to treatment for Mrs. B., the widowed wife who presented 2 months after the death of her husband with moderately severe symptoms at the outset, was conservative and stepwise, starting with psychotherapy. I believe education was vital to the success of her treatment. During the first part of treatment, when her depressive symptoms were subsyndromal, she requested the use of an antidepressant drug. I urged her to monitor with me the course of the symptoms for a period of 2 months during which the symptoms subsided spontaneously. Mrs. B. needed strong encouragement to face the feared aspects of her loss and it took 3 separate treatment efforts to finally get to the core trauma over the sudden, unexpected, frightening death of her husband. The second and third parts of treatment began near the anniversaries of her husband's death. In the third part of treatment, a careful, minute review of the circumstances of her husband's death seemed to provide a desensitization experience for her. It was on completion of this process that a more coherent story of her loss and its consequences was accomplished. Eventually, she had a complex array of symptoms including panic, depressive symptoms, and a phobia of flying in airplanes. In retrospect, I might have been more vigorous about extending the first part of treatment if I had relied more on the evaluation of the risk factors for her. With regard to the use of psychotropic drugs, my efforts to treat her depressive symptoms in the second period of treatment may have contributed to the reoccurrence of nighttime panic attacks, an unintended consequence and the cause of abandoning the antidepressants.

Interpretation of the identification symptom was particularly useful to turn a corner in therapy with Mrs. C., the bereaved, adult daughter. She felt orphaned by the death of her mother and had many unresolved issues to deal with stemming from her father's death when she was a teenage girl. Much time was spent in reviewing and clarifying the long history of her relationship to her mother. In particular, Mrs. C. felt her mother had not supported her adequately when her father died. When I eventually interpreted her self-critical attitude as an identification symptom regarding her mother, it seemed to provide impetus for her to move on to other current relationships to her brother and husband and move to a conclusion. The effective use of antidepressant medication provided relief of depressive symptoms and a foundation for addressing her intense grief as well as the complex relationship issues in her treatment. Clarifying some of her problems of self-esteem as a function of the depression, rather than a cause of her illness, provided an alternative perspective that was useful to this woman.

Mr. D. was flooded with horrific images of the violent death of his daughter and felt overwhelmed by his fear and rage. In contrast to Mrs. B., he needed assistance in taking more distance, consoling himself, and constructing an understanding of the death that he could live with. Intermittently, I would encourage him to confront the aggravating aspects of the trial of his daughter's murderer. It seemed to me that education about the separation distress and the traumatic distress he was experiencing helped him to gain some mastery over his experience and his life. The use of antidepressants to relieve his depressive symptoms and in particular to help establish a more normal sleep pattern helped him gain more of a sense of control. Successful antidepressant treatment also reinforced my efforts to help him understand that he had not failed his daughter and that his feelings of guilt, a nagging symptom that plagued him, were a product of the depressive illness.

☐ Conclusion

The diagnosis/treatment algorithm and my personal notes on treatment are intended to help integrate and illustrate some of the more technical discussion and review of treatments in chapters 3, 4, and 5. Although there are core elements in all treatments, each treatment plan is unique. The algorithm and discussion are intended to illustrate how treatment should be implemented at the proper level of intensity and within an appropriate, individualized treatment plan for each patient while being sensitive to natural processes of recovery and attending to the person who is ill.

☐ References

Beck, A. T., Rush, A. J., Shaw, B. F., & Emery, G. (1979). *Cognitive therapy of depression.* New York: Guilford Press.

Clayton, P. J., Halikas, J. A., & Maurice, W. L. (1971). The bereavement of the widowed. *Diseases of the Nervous System, 32,* 597–604.

Horowitz, M.,. Marmar, C., Krupnick, J., Wilner, N., Kaltreider, N., & Wallerstein, R. (1984). *Personality styles and brief psychotherapy.* New York: Basic Books.

Jacobs, S. (1993). *Pathologic grief: Maladaptation to loss.* Washington, DC: American Psychiatric Press.

Jacobs, S., Kasl, S., Schaefer, C.,. & Ostfeld, A. (1994). Conscious and unconscious coping with loss. *Psychosomatic Medicine, 56,* 557–563.

Jacobs, S., & Prigerson, H. G. (1996). Problem focused, integrated psychotherapy for complicated grief. *In Session: Psychotherapy in Practice, 2,* 21–30.

Klass, D. (Ed.). (1996). *Continuing bonds: New understanding of grief.* Washington, DC: Taylor and Francis.

Klerman, G. L., Weissman, M. M., Rounsaville, B. J., & Chevron, (1984). *Interpersonal psychotherapy of depression.* New York: Basic Books.

Peabody, F. W. (1977). The care of the patient. *Psychiatric Annals, 7,* 264–273.

Prigerson, H. G., Maciejewski, P. K., Newsom, J., Reynolds, C. F., Frank, E., Bierhals, A. J., Miller, M. D., Fasiczka, A., Doman, J., Houck, P. R. (1995). The inventory of complicated grief: A scale to measure maladaptive symptoms of loss. *Psychiatry Research, 59,* 65–79.

Pynoos, R. S., & Nader, K. (1993). Issues in the treatment of posttraumatic stress in children and adolescents. In J. P. Wilson, & B. Raphael, (Eds.), The international handbook of traumatic stress syndromes. New York: Plenum Press.

Rando, T. A. (1993). *Treatment of complicated mourning.* Champaign, Ill: Research Press.

Raphael, B., Middleton, W., Martinek, N., & Misso, V. (1993). Counseling and therapy of the bereaved. In M. S. Stroebe, W. Stroebe, & R. O. Hansson (Eds.), Handbook of bereavement: Theory, research, and intervention (pp. 427–453). Cambridge, England: Cambridge University Press.

Rynearson, E. K. (1996). Psychotherapy of bereavement after homicide: Be offensive. *In Session: Psychotherapy in Practice, 2*, 47–57.

Shuchter, S. R., Downs, N., & Zisook, S. (1996). *Biologically informed psychotherapy for depression.* New York: Guilford Publications.

Tucker, G. (1998). Putting DSM-IV in perspective (editorial). *American Journal of Psychiatry, 155*, 159–161.

Zisook, S., Shuchter, S. R. (1996). Psychotherapy of the depressions in spousal bereavement. *In Session: Psychotherapy in Practice, 2*, 31–45.

Epidemiology and Prevention of Traumatic Grief

The working, diagnostic criteria for Traumatic Grief are new, so studies of the epidemiology of Traumatic Grief are limited in number. Therefore, using a similar strategy to that adopted in the case of discussing some of the associated diagnostic features in chapter 3, I will draw on the literature regarding pathologic grief. I include studies that antedate the development of the new diagnostic criteria and are based on definitions of a disorder that vary from the criteria for Traumatic Grief. A caveat for the reader is that many of the conclusions discussed here and based on varying definitions of pathologic grief will need to be verified in studies using the new criteria. At the same time I suspect that many, if not most, of the variables identified in the following discussion will be confirmed.

☐ Prevalence and Incidence of Traumatic Grief

Estimates of the prevalence rate of pathologic range from 14 to 34% (Dimond, Lund, & Caserta, 1987; Lazare, 1979; Maddison and Viola, 1968; Parkes, 1970; Parkes & Weiss, 1983; Vachon et al., 1982; Zisook & DeVaul, 1983; Zisook, Shuchter, & Shuckit, 1985). These estimates vary depending on the definition of pathologic grief and the time framework chosen for study. None of these prevalence estimates derive from large epidemiologic data sets. Recently, two Australian studies estimated the rate of chronic grief, which is only one variant of pathologic grief, to be 9.2% in a general adult population (Middleton, Burnett, Raphael, & Martinek, 1996) and 8.8% among elderly widowers (Byrne & Raphael, 1994). In these two community based, small to medium sized samples of bereaved persons, the rarity of exposure to violent or threatening circumstances of death may have limited the observation of delayed variants of pathologic grief. This is true because sudden, unexpected, violent deaths are linked to delayed grief (Middleton et al., 1996). The discrepancies above among the estimates of prevalence rates need to be resolved through more studies using epidemiologic strategies. Still, even if future data come in at the low or middle range of the above estimates, the prevalence of Traumatic Grief is substantial.

Given the estimate of a high prevalence of Traumatic Grief, the use of the consensus diagnostic criteria in screening for incident cases of the disorder could become an important first step in addressing a significant mental health problem. For example, in 1993, 2,268,533 deaths were registered in the United States each leaving at least two bereaved family members, or 4,537,066 bereaved persons annually (National Center for Health Statistics, 1996). Precise nosology, timely screening, and clinical diagnosis would facilitate early detection and intervention for the approximately 20% of these bereaved persons (this is a crude, midrange figure taken from the above prevalence estimates) who develop incident cases of Traumatic Grief.

Another, indirect perspective on the incidence of Traumatic Grief comes from published rates of the death of a significant other, a cornerstone event that opens a period of risk for the development of Traumatic Grief. In a representative, community study of Kentucky adults, Murrell and colleagues estimated that 14% of women and 12% of men experience a death in the family each year (Murrell, Norris, & Hutchins, 1984a). Recently, in another community survey, Breslau and colleagues estimated that 60% of an urban population of 18- to 45-year-old persons had experienced the death of a significant other sometime during their lifetime (Breslau et al., 1988). In an older population, the rate would presumably approximate 100%. What is notable in this study is how high it is for younger and middle aged adults. The rates of death of significant others suggest the incidence of Traumatic Grief may be high. Nevertheless, instead of these indirect perspectives, we need more direct and precise estimates of the incidence of Traumatic Grief from epidemiologic studies using standardized assessments to clarify the magnitude of the problem for society. Studies of incidence will also clarify risk factors for Traumatic Grief, which are discussed below.

☐ Age and Gender Variation in Grief and Traumatic Grief

There are no differences by age and sex among adults in the intensity of separation distress (Jacobs, Kasl, Ostfeld, Berkman, Charpentiér, 1986). On the other hand, elderly bereaved persons react to a death with less emotional numbness and disbelief than a middle aged comparison group (Jacobs, Kasl, Ostfeld, Berkman, Charpentiér, 1986). Item analyses verify that symptoms of Traumatic Grief occur in all adult age groups, including young adults, and are distinct from depressive and anxious symptoms (Prigerson et al., 1995a, and b; Prigerson, Bierhals, Kasla, Reynolds, & Shear, 1996).

Several clinical reports indicate that young bereaved persons are at high risk for pathologic grief (Jacobs & Kim, 1990; Jacobs, 1993). Corresponding to these reports, in a recent analysis of a sample ranging in age from 45 to 87 years old, younger age is a risk factor for Traumatic Grief (Prigerson, unpublished paper). While the risk of developing Traumatic Grief is high for younger persons, the frequency of death is still greatest among the elderly, thus creating for them an elevated risk of exposure to a loss compared to younger counterparts.

Bereaved women report more numbness and disbelief and more depressive and neurovegetative symptoms during bereavement than men however, no gender difference in the intensity of separation distress is observed in the general, bereaved population (Jacobs et al., 1986). Some observers have reported a higher risk of pathologic grief among bereaved women (Zisook & De Vaul, 1983). Recent, cross sectional (Bierhals et al., 1995) and longitudinal analyses of Traumatic Grief (Chen et al., in press) show that the disorder, Traumatic Grief, occurs in both bereaved men and women and that widows report more intense symptoms of Traumatic Grief than widowers for five years after a death.

☐ Social and Cultural Issues

Cross cultural studies document that grief is essentially universal after the death of a significant other (Krupp & Kligfeld, 1962; Mathison, 1970; Rosenblatt, 1993). Systematic, clinical studies differentiating normal grief from pathologic grief and supporting the universality of a disorder associated with grief have appeared from the United States (Zisook & Shuchter, 1993; Prigerson et al., 1995a; Bierhals et al., 1995; Wortman & Silver, 1989; Zisook & De Vaul, 1977; Clayton, Desmarais, & Winokur, 1968), Britain (Bowlby, 1980; Parkes, 1970; Parkes, 1972), Canada (Vachon et al., 1982), Germany (Stroebe & Stroebe, 1991, 1993), Holland (Kleber & Brom, 1987;

Cleiren, de Keijser, van den Bout, & Dijhuis), Sweden (Lundin, 1984, 1987; Grimby, 1993), Israel (Elizur & Kaffman, 1980; Levav, 1989; Roskin, 1984; Rubin, 1992), Japan (Yamamoto, 1969), Australia (Middleton, Moylan, Raphael, Burnett, & Martinek, 1993); Middleton et al., 1996; Byrne & Raphael, 1994; Raphael, 1989; Raphael & Middleton, 1990), and Chile (Becker et al., 1989). These studies form a preliminary basis for the premise articulated in the Preface that the consensus diagnostic criteria for Traumatic Grief have universal utility and cut across social and cultural boundaries. This broad, cross cultural documentation also serves as a cornerstone for the assumption that the absence of grief after the death of a significant other is notable and may connote a maladaptive reaction to a death.

Assuming that a premise about the universality of Traumatic Grief is true, it is important to point out that the expression of the symptoms of Traumatic Grief might occur in different forms depending on social and cultural attitudes. Even in the most homogenized, modern, industrial, bmetropolitan communities, many persons, in particular new immigrants, identify with and preserve some primary ethnic identify and this shapes, in part, the clinical picture. For example, in a culture that discourages emotional expression, a person might meet criteria according to some of the less emotional and more cognitive, behavioral, and avoidant elements of diagnosis in Criterion B. In such a culture, somatic symptoms might be prominent and overshadow the consensus criteria. As another example, social and cultural prescriptions for facing adversity with a stoic attitude, such as the stiff, upper lipped Yankee, might lead to an overall suppression of the primarily emotional and psychological criteria for diagnosis in Criteria A and B. The consequence of this for diagnosis might be a muted report of the severity of symptoms by a bereaved person, leading to a mistaken decision to ignore a disorder. In a culture that encourages emotional expression, such as some southern European countries, the opposite might occur. If cultural attitudes were to amplify the expression and intensity of symptoms, it would be important to establish appropriate cut-offs for that culture or focus on some of the less emotional cognitive, behavioral and avoidant criteria. The sophisticated clinician ought to take this social and cultural variation into account when making a diagnosis of Traumatic Grief.

The social and cultural background of a person shapes in part his or her response to bereavement in other ways too (Rosenblatt, 1993). Society accords special status and roles to the bereaved and prescribes mourning rituals to follow when bereavement occurs. Interaction with other people helps bereaved persons find a meaning in bereavement as they create their story about the loss and their survival. These social processes of bereavement can be attenuated in some communities and in the circumstances of rapid social change in societies that find themselves in the midst of accelerated urban and industrial development.

Conventional wisdom among clinicians who see bereaved patients is that the breakdown of stable communities, the attenuation of extended families, and the homogenization of popular culture in modern, industrial society makes it harder for bereaved persons to cope. At the same time, these changes place a new burden on professional persons who are sought out by bereaved persons who develop problems and need help. There is some truth in this conventional wisdom. I believe it is part of the background for the development of diagnostic criteria for Traumatic Grief. Rapid social change in American society over the past century roughly corresponds with a growing professional concern with the problems of bereavement. Southern tier countries undergoing rapid development or any country experiencing rapid transition from agrarian, small town life to an industrial or postindustrial economy may be recapitulating the change witnessed in American society over the past 100 years.

If professionals take on responsibility for helping bereaved persons, it is incumbent on them to become aware of social and cultural variations in bereavement practices (Parkes, 1993). Some social prescriptions are useful such as funerals and anniversary observances that help the bereaved person come to terms with a death. Other social prescriptions may not be helpful, such as rigid expectations about when grief should be over, insistence on resumption of an old role, or perpetuating a lifeless memory. In evaluation and treatment, opportunities occur to question, support, and take advantage, when appropriate, of these social processes. Ignoring them can contribute to the damage to these social processes, already underway in the circumstances of rapid social change in modern society. In addition, ignoring them runs the risk of alienating both bereaved persons and their families from the caregiver.

The primary unit of society is the family. Consistent with this discussion of social and cultural variation, it is important for clinicians to remember the family context of bereavement. Within a bereaved family, members may grieve differently and progress at different rates placing strain on the family unit. Family meetings can be useful to clarify these issues and help in problem solving (Black, 1979; Kosten, Jacobs, & Kasl, 1985).

☐ Utilization of Services and Costs

Efficient screening, diagnosis, and treatment for Traumatic Grief can reduce the societal costs of bereavement by curbing the nonspecific, secondary use of health care services and the personal costs and suffering associated with this disorder.

Prigerson and colleagues have begun an exploratory study that compares health utilization and its associated costs of bereaved persons with high versus low levels of Traumatic Grief symptoms at 6 months after a death in a sample of 154 widowed persons (Prigerson, Rosenheck, Jacobs, unpublished data). The preliminary results reveal that Traumatic Grief symptoms are significantly and positively associated with increased hospitalizations ($r = .11$, $p < .04$), number of days spent in the hospital ($r = .35$, $p < .001$), and number of physician visits ($r = .35$, $p < .01$). A summary measure of health costs was created by multiplying units of service, such as hospital days or physician visits, by estimated unit costs, such as dollars per day or per visit. These costs were then summed to generate total point-in-time estimates of service costs during the 7 months prior to the 6 month interview. In these preliminary analyses, they found that Traumatic Grief symptoms at 6 months are a highly significant predictor of health care costs at 13 months postintake (coefficient = 4.21, $p < .01$), controlling for depression, interaction of traumatic grief and depression, sex, age, health insurance coverage and baseline, self-rated health. They also found that those with a Traumatic Grief score in the upper 20% of the distribution have a significantly higher, mean health care cost of $2,004 versus $595 among those below that threshold at the 6 month assessment ($p < .0001$). While these results suggest a close association between Traumatic Grief and health care utilization and costs, the dataset available for this study had neither a thorough assessment of health care use nor information on whether subjects met criteria for a diagnosis of Traumatic Grief, using instead a symptom score. Thus, the association between health service use and the consensus diagnostic criteria for Traumatic Grief awaits validation from analyses of better data.

☐ Risk Factors for Traumatic Grief

Traumatic Grief is a disorder that is specifically related to the environmental absence created by the death of a significant other. As this disorder is ecologically specific, it raises the possibility of not only personal but also environmental risk factors. Multiaxial assessments, as in DSM-IV, enables documentation of both person and environmental risk factors, establishing a comprehensive framework for the evaluation of risk factors for each patient.

   Implicit in the definition of an ecologically specific disorder is the idea that a socioenvironmental event, a death, opens a period of risk for exposed persons. It is possible that the mode of death may augment the risk. Indeed, there is evidence that sudden and unexpected deaths (which are often untimely) and suicidal and violent deaths (which are typically sudden and unexpected) increase the risk of symptoms of pathologic grief

(Jacobs, 1993; Parkes & Weiss, 1983; Zisook & Lyons, 1989; Lundin, 1984, 1987; Ball, 1977; Lehman, Wortman, & Williams, 1987; Sanders, 1989). The data are not uniform on this question, particularly among the elderly for whom chronic illness before a death is associated with more difficult bereavement (Breckenridge, Gallagher, Thompson, Peterson, 1986; Heyman & Gianturco, 1973; Maddison & Walker, 1967). Multiple losses, sometimes referred to as bereavement overload (Kastenbaum, 1969), also augment risk (Parkes, 1991).

Among personal risk factors, young age and female gender of the bereaved have been considered risk factors. This is supported in a recent study of Traumatic Grief (Prigerson et al., 1995b). In addition, kinship makes a difference. Bereaved spouses, parents, adolescents, and possibly adult sisters of older brothers are at higher risk for problematic grief than persons with other relationships to the deceased (Sanders, 1980, 1989; Cleiren, 1991). Also, although the terms for definition of an attachment disturbance vary from author to author (ambivalence, existence of latent self-images and role models, insecure attachment), the generic risk factor of an attachment disturbance is consistently identified as a risk factor throughout the past century (Freud, 1953; Bowlby, 1969; Horowitz, Wilner, & Marmar, 1980). Personality traits such as dependency (Parkes & Weiss, 1983), schizoid personality on the Minnesota Multiphase Personality Inventory (MMPI) (Sanders, 1989), and high ratings of neuroticism (Jacobs et al., 1985) also may establish a higher risk for pathologic grief. Finally, childhood losses, particularly in the absence of adequate substitutive nurturance (Tennant, 1988), probably create permanent neurobiologic changes, affect a person's attachment style, and pose higher risk of difficulty with deaths that occur in adulthood.

In addition to these trait variables, there is some evidence of state variables as personal risk factors. These include inability of a family member to accept an imminent death (Parkes & Weiss, 1983) or severe distress of a family member during the terminal illness of a family member who dies (Schut et al., 1991; Hays, Kasl, & Jacobs, 1994).

The profile of risk factors for Traumatic Grief that emerges from these studies contains elements that are different from risk factor profiles for other major psychiatric disorders. To the extent that this risk factor profile proves to be particular to Traumatic Grief in subsequent studies using the consensus diagnostic criteria and in epidemiologic studies of the incidence of the disorder, the unique epidemiologic profile can be added to the evidence discussed in chapter 2 as support for the concept of Traumatic Grief as a distinct disorder.

☐ Prevention of Traumatic Grief

The nature of Traumatic Grief as a disorder associated with the death of a significant other, which is a specific, easily identifiable event in a person's life, provides a unique opportunity for preventive interventions (Jacobs, 1993). Nevertheless, evidence to support recommendations for the prevention of Traumatic Grief, given the recent development of the nosologic concept, is quite limited. Still, clinicians would be remiss if they missed the opportunity to review what is known and, employing our existing knowledge of risk factors, think about the task of prevention.

The prevalence figures discussed above, taken together with the findings of studies of psychosocial stressors that regularly rank bereavement as the most stressful event in a person's life (Holmes & Rahe, 1968; Paykel, Prusoff, & Uhlenhuth, 1971; Murrell et al., 1984b), argue in favor of the development of preventive programs to address the disorders spawned by deaths in the family or among intimate friends of the deceased. This point of view is buttressed by a contemporary upsurge in the number of deaths from violent causes, which may increase the risk for Traumatic Grief (Rando, 1993).

Public health workers recognize three types of prevention. Primary prevention involves elimination of, or protection from, the causes of disease. Spraying for mosquitoes that are vectors of disease and vaccinations are examples of primary prevention. Success is measured by a reduction in new cases or the incidence of a disorder. Secondary prevention involves early, efficient treatment intervention for incipient illness. Screening programs for hypertension or breast cancer are examples of secondary prevention. Success is measured in this case by reducing mortality, morbidity, and disability that are consequences of a disorder. Tertiary prevention involves prompt rehabilitation and health education for persons with a disease who are disabled. Physical and occupational therapies for poststroke or postcoronary patients are an example of tertiary prevention which is measured by a reduction in rates of disability.

Although we need more data on risk factors for Traumatic Grief using the consensus diagnostic criteria, it would appear from existing knowledge that there are opportunities for primary prevention. For example, unexpected deaths are associated with a higher risk of poor outcomes (Lundin, 1984). Moreover, Parkes and Weiss observed that a sudden death was associated with pathologic grief in a study of young adult widows (Parkes & Weiss, 1983). These observations place emphasis on the needs of surviving family members and providing them an opportunity to take leave of a patient before death occurs. When this is impossible in the circumstances of a sudden death, an alternative after the death has occurred is to provide an opportunity for a family or intimates to spend time with the deceased person in a quiet place or offer crisis intervention for high risk, bereaved family members to avert the onset of Traumatic Grief. The psychiatric consultant in a general hospital or emergency room is particularly well placed to take action on these interventions. In addition, social policies and programs that fall outside the principal domain of clinical practice, such as gun control initiatives, campaigns against drinking and driving, and conflict mediation programs to avert violence, serve as examples of primary prevention if they lead to a reduction in the rate of violent, unnatural deaths.

The availability of the Traumatic Grief Evaluation of Response to Loss (TRGER2L) (available from Prigerson on request), a screening instrument for Traumatic Grief derived from the Inventory for Complicated Grief (ICG) (Prigerson et al., 1995b), provides an opportunity for secondary prevention. By systematically screening high risk populations of bereaved persons, such as senior widowers who have a high risk for suicide, it would be possible to intervene early in the course of a disorder and prevent not only prolonged morbidity but also perhaps mortality from suicide. Responsibility for screening for diseases traditionally falls in the province of public health officers. Nevertheless, psychiatrists have progressively taken initiative in this arena in the form of depression screening or anxiety screening days in the community during mental illness awareness weeks or mental health awareness months.

Long term therapies and mutual support interventions hold potential for reducing the persistent impairments in interpersonal and psychosocial functioning that can occur when the diagnosis of Traumatic Grief is missed and a chronic course of illness is established. These are good examples of tertiary prevention. Difficult anniversaries are often milestones that motivate patients to seek help from clinicians late in the course of illness when disability is established. In addition, candidates for tertiary prevention can be picked up in screening programs after the opportunity for secondary prevention has been missed.

All these opportunities for prevention provide incentive for the systematic testing of preventive interventions, which warrant the attention of clinicians who want to achieve a comprehensive approach to caring for patients with Traumatic Grief.

☐ Conclusion

Given that the diagnosis of Traumatic Grief is anchored in the death of a significant other, an event that is easily identifiable and that is included in public health statistics, now that diagnostic criteria are available, there is an opportunity to develop a precise and useful epidemiology of Traumatic Grief. I have argued above that the incidence and prevalence of Traumatic Grief is substantial. The magnitude of Traumatic Grief as a public health and clinical problem deserves our attention. When data from systematic screening of representative populations and preventive interventions for Traumatic Grief become available, the clinician will have the tools to make some of the most efficient and effective preventive interventions possible in psychiatry. Then clinicians will be able to engage in "the ultimate business of health professionals," that is, the prevention and control of a disorder (Susser, 1981, p. 7).

I believe bereaved persons are increasingly turning to professional help in societies characterized by rapid social change and accompanying attenuation of the power of social processes of bereavement. When bereaved persons seek help it is important for the helping professionals to fulfill their roles as healers, not only by providing wise professional advice and care but also by learning about social and cultural variation in the expression of grief and supporting the social rituals that contribute to healing of the individual, bereaved person.

☐ References

Ball, J. F. (1977). Widow's grief: The impact of age and mode of death. *Omega, 7,* 307–333.

Becker, D., Castillo, M. I., Gomez, E., Kovalsky, J., et al. (1989). Subjectivity and politics: The psychotherapy of extreme traumatization in Chile. *International Journal of Mental Health, 18,* 80–97.

Bierhals, A. J., Prigerson, H. G., Frank, E., Reynolds, C. F., Fasiczka, A., & Miller, M. D. (1995). Gender differences in complicated grief among the elderly. *Omega, 32,* 303–317.

Black, D. (1979). The bereaved child. *Journal of Child Psychiatry and Psychology, 19,* 287–292.

Bowlby, J. (1969). *Attachment and loss, vol 1: Attachment.* New York: Basic Books.

Bowlby, J. (1980). *Attachment and loss, vol 3: Loss, sadness, and depression.* New York: Basic Books.

Breckenridge, J. N., Gallagher, D., Thompson, L. W., Peterson, J. (1986). Characteristic depressive symptoms of bereaved elders. *Journal of Gerontology, 41,* 163–168.

Breslau, N., Kessler, R. C., Chilcoat, H. D., Schultz, L. R., Davis, G. C., & Andreski, P. (1998). Trauma and Post-traumatic Stress Disorder in the community. *Archives of General Psychiatry, 55,* 626–632.

Byrne, G. J. A., & Raphael, B. (1994). The psychological symptoms of conjugal bereavement in elderly men over the first 13 months. *Psychological Medicine, 24,* 411–421.

Chen, J. H., Bierhals, A. J., Prigerson, H. G., Kasl, S. V., Mazure, C., & Jacobs, S. C. (in press). Gender differences in the effects of bereavement-related psychological distress on health outcomes. *Psychological Medicine.*

Clayton, P. J., Desmarais, L., & Winokur, G. (1968). A study of normal bereavement. *American Journal of Psychiatry, 125,* 168–178.

Cleiren, M.P.H.D. (1991). *Adaptation after bereavement.* Leiden, Holland: DSWO Press.

Dimond, M., Lund, D. A., & Caserta, M. S. (1987). The role of social support in the first two years of bereavement in an elderly sample. *The Gerontologist, 27,* 599–604.

Elizur, E., & Kaffman, M. (1980). Children's bereavement reactions following the death of the father. *Journal of the American Academy of Child Psychiatry, 21,* 474–480.

Freud, S. (1953). Mourning and melancholia. In J. Strackey (Ed. and Trans.), The standard edition, volume 14 (pp. 243–285). London: Hogarth.

Grimby, A. (1993). Bereavement among elderly people: Grief reactions, post-bereavement hallucinations and quality of life. *Acta Psychiatrica Scandinavica, 87,* 72–80.

Hays, J. C., Kasl, S. V., & Jacobs, S. C. (1994). The course of psychological distress following threatened and actual conjugal bereavement. *Psychological Medicine, 24,* 917–927.

Heyman, D. K., & Gianturco, D. T. (1973). Long term adaptation by the elderly to bereavement. *Journal of Gerontology, 28,* 259–262.

Holmes, T. H., & Rahe, R. H. (1968). The social readjustment rating scale. *Journal of Psychosomatic Research, 11,* 213–218.

Horowitz, M. J., Wilner, N., & Marmar, C. (1980). Pathological grief and the activation of latent self-images. *American Journal of Psychiatry, 137,* 1157–1162.

Jacobs, S., Mason, J., Kosten, T., Kasl, S., Ostfeld, A., Atkins, S., Gardner, C., & Schreiber, S. (1985). Acute bereavement, threatened loss, ego defenses, and adrenocortical function. *Psychotherapy and Psychosomatics, 44,* 151–159.

Jacobs, S. C., Kasl, S. V., Ostfeld, A. M., Berkman, L., Charpentiér, P. (1986). The measurement of grief: Age and sex variation. *Journal of Medical Psychology, 59,* 305–310.

Jacobs, S., Kim, K. (1990). Psychiatric complications of bereavement. *Psychiatric Annals, 20,* 314–317.

Jacobs, S. (1993). *Pathologic grief: Maladaptation to loss.* Washington, DC: American Psychiatric Press.

Kastenbaum, R. (1969). Death and bereavement in later life. In A. Kutcher (Ed.), *Death and bereavement.* (pp. 28–54). Springfield, Ill: Charles C. Thomas.

Kleber, R. J., & Brom, D. (1987). Psychotherapy and pathological grief controlled outcome study. *Israel Journal of Psychiatry & Related Sciences, 24,* 99–109.

Kosten, T. R., Jacobs, S. C., Kasl, S. V. (1985). Terminal illness, bereavement, and the family. In D. C. Tuck, & R. D. Kerns, (Eds.), *Health, illness, and families.* (pp. 311–337). New York: Wiley.

Krupp, G. R., & Kligfeld, B. (1962). The bereavement reaction: A cross cultural evaluation. *Journal of Religion and Health, 1,* 222–246.

Lazare, A. (1979). Unresolved grief. In A Lazare (Ed.), Outpatient psychiatry: Diagnosis and treatment. (pp. 498–512). Baltimore: Williams and Wilkins.

Lehman, D. R., Wortman, C. B., & Williams, A. F. (1987). Long term effects of losing a spouse or child in a motor vehicle accident. *Journal of Personal and Social Psychiatry, 52,* 218–231.

Levav, I. (1989). Second thoughts on the lethal aftermath of a loss. *Omega, 20,* 81–90.

Lundin, T. (1984). Morbidity following sudden and unexpected bereavement. *British Journal of Psychiatry, 144,* 84–88.

Lundin, T. (1987). The stress of unexpected bereavement. *Stress Medicine, 3,* 109–114.

Maddison, D. C., & Walker, W. L. (1967). Factors affecting the outcome of conjugal bereavement. *British Journal of Psychiatry, 113,* 1057–1067.

Maddison, D., & Viola, A. (1968). The health of widows in the year following bereavement. *Journal of Psychosomatic Research, 12,* 297–306.

Mathison, J. (1970). A cross cultural view of widowhood. *Omega, 1,* 201–218.

Middleton, W., Moylan, A., Raphael, B., Burnett, P., Martinek, N. (1993). An international perspective on bereavement related concepts. *Australian and New Zealand Journal of Psychiatry, 27,* 457–463.

Middleton, W., Burnett, P., Raphael, B., & Martinek, N. (1996). The bereavement response—a cluster analysis. *British Journal of Psychiatry, 169,* 167–171.

Murrell, S. A., Norris, F. H., Hutchins, G. L. (1984a). Distribution and desirability of life events in older adults: Population and policy implications. *Journal of Community Psychology, 12,* 301–311.

National Center for Health Statistics. (1996). Advance report of final mortality statistics, 1993. *Monthly Vital Statistics Report,* Suppl.

Parkes, C. M. (1970). The first year of bereavement: A longitudinal study of the reaction of London widows to the death of their husbands. *Psychiatry, 33,* 449–467.

Parkes, C. M. (1972). *Bereavement: Studies of grief in adult life.* New York: International Universities Press.

Parkes, C. M., Weiss, R. S. (1983). *Recovery from bereavement.* New York: Basic Books.

Parkes, C. M. (1991). Risk factors in bereavement: Implications for prevention and treatment of pathologic grief. *Psychiatric Annals, 20,* 308–310.

Parkes, C. M. (1993). Bereavement as a psychosocial transition: Processes of adaptation to change. In M. S. Stroebe, W. Stroebe, & R. O. Hansson, (Eds.), New York: Cambridge University Press.

Paykel, E. S., Prusoff, B. A., & Uhlenhuth, E. H. (1971). Scaling of life events. *Archives of General Psychiatry, 15,* 340–347.

Prigerson, H. G., Frank, E., Kasl, S. V., Reynolds, C. F., Anderson, B., Zubenko, G. S., Houck, P. R., George, C. J., & Kupfer, D. J. (1995a). Complicated grief and bereavement-related depression as distinct disorders: Preliminary empirical validation in elderly bereaved spouses. *American Journal of Psychiatry, 152,* 22–30.

Prigerson, H. G., Maciejewski, P. K., Newsom, J., Reynolds, C. F., Frank, E., Bierhals, A. J., Miller, M. D., Fasiczka, A., Doman, J., & Houck, P. R. (1995b). The inventory of complicated grief: A scale to measure maladaptive symptoms of loss. *Psychiatry Research, 59,* 65–79.

Prigerson, H. G., Bierhals, A. J., Kasl, S. V., Reynolds, C. F., & Shear, M. K. Disorder from bereavement-related depression and anxiety: A replication study. *The American Journal of Psychiatry, 153,* 1484–1486.

Rando, T. A. (1993). *Treatment of complicated mourning.* Champaign, IL: Research Press.

Raphael, B. (1989, May). *Diagnostic criteria for bereavement reactions.* Paper presented at the International Symposium on Pathological Bereavement, Seattle, WA.

Raphael, B., Middleton, W. (1990). What is pathologic grief? *Psychiatric Annals, 20,* 304–307.

Rosenblatt, P. C. (1993). The social context of private feelings. In M. S. Stroebe, W. Stroebe, & R. O. Hansson, (Eds.). Handbook of bereavement: Theory, research, and intervention, (pp. 102–111). New York: Cambridge University Press.

Roskin, M. (1984). Emotional reactions among bereaving Israeli parents. *Israel Journal of Psychiatry & Related Sciences, 21,* 73–84.

Rubin, S. (1992). Adult child loss and two-track model of bereavement. *Omega, 24,* 183–202.

Sanders, C. M. (1980). A comparison of adult bereavement in the death of a spouse, child, and parent. *Omega, 10,* 303–322.

Sanders, C. M. (1989). Grief: *The mourning after.* New York: Wiley.

Schut, H. A. W., de Keijser, J., van den Bout, J., & Dijhuis, J. H. (1991). Post-traumatic symptoms in the first year of conjugal bereavement. *Anxiety Research, 4,* 225–234.

Stroebe, M., & Stroebe, W. (1991). Does "grief work" work? *Journal of Consulting and Clinical Psychology, 59,* 479–482.

Stroebe, M. S., & Stroebe, W. (1993). The mortality of bereavement. In M. S. Stroebe, W. Stroebe, & R. O. Hansson (Eds.), *Handbook of bereavement: Theory, research, and intervention.* (pp. 175–195). New York: Cambridge University Press.

Susser, M. (1981). The epidemiology of life stress. *Psychological Medicine, 11,* 1–8.

Tennant, C. (1988). parental loss in childhood. *Archives of General Psychiatry, 45,* 1045–1050.

Vachon, M. L. S., Sheldon, A. R., Lancee, W. J., Lyall, W. A. L., Rogers, J., & Freeman, S. J. J. (1982). Correlates of enduring distress patterns following bereavement: Social network, life situation, and personality. *Psychological Medicine, 12,* 783–788.

Wortman, C. B., & Silver, R. C. (1989). The myths of coping with loss. *Journal of Consulting and Clinical Psychology, 57,* 349–357.

Yamamoto, J., Okonogi, K., Iwasaki, T., & Yoshimura, S. (1969). Mourning in Japan. *American Journal of Psychiatry, 125,* 1660–1665.

Zisook, S., & De Vaul, R. A. (1977). Grief related facsimile illness. *International Journal of Psychiatry Medicine, 7,* 329–336.

Zisook, S., & De Vaul, R. A. (1983). Grief, unresolved grief, and depression. *Psychosomatics, 24,* 247–256.

Zisook, S., Shuchter, S., & Schuckit, M. (1985). Factors in the persistence of unresolved grief among psychiatric outpatients. *Psychosomatics, 26,* 497–503.

Zisook, S., & Lyons, L. (1989). Bereavement and unresolved in psychiatric outpatients. *Omega, 20,* 307–322.

Zisook, S., & Shuchter, S. R. (1993). Uncomplicated bereavement. *Journal of Clinical Psychiatry, 54, 365–372.*

8
CHAPTER

Conclusion and Future Directions

☐ The Costs and Benefits of Attachment

The insight by Bowlby and others that human social relationships serve an essential biologic function and confer evolutionary advantage set the stage for a modern understanding of grief (Bowlby, 1969). Our highly developed capacity for affiliation sets us apart from other species and grief is an intrinsic human response to a separation or loss of a significant other. Separation distress serves the purpose of maintaining or regaining the relationship to the absent, presumably protective attachment figure. We appreciate this poignantly when a child is separated from his mother or father. While commitment is a potential source of dysphoria in the circumstances of a loss, it is also a source of fundamental gratification and satisfaction. It is well to remind ourselves of this after dwelling so long through this text on Traumatic Grief, the psychopathologic side of attachment. We know the joys of attachment as the experience of falling in love, the pleasure of enduring commitments, the enjoyment of the comforts of home, and the gratification of intimate friendships with others. Thus, attachment is a source of enormous satisfaction as well as potential distress. As Parkes reminded us, grief is "the cost of commitment" (Parkes, 1972).

☐ The Clinical Challenge

When the normal process of grief goes off track and clinical complications occur, and particularly when a bereaved person seeks expert advice, it is the responsibility of clinicians to recognize and relieve, if possible, the suffering of the bereaved person. The goals of this book are to enhance the recognition of Traumatic Grief as a clinical complication of bereavement through informed diagnosis (chapters 2 and 3) and to encourage the application of specific, targeted treatments and preventive interventions for it (chapters 5, 6, and 7).

☐ Review of the Text

Unifying two historical views on pathologic grief, recent factor analyses of data from both clinical and community based samples provide evidence of a unidimensional factor that incorporates symptoms of separation anxiety that are provoked by the death of a significant other with symptoms of traumatic distress that reflect feelings of devastation caused by the death. In chapter 2, based on the recent recommendations of a diagnostic consensus conference for Traumatic Grief (Prigerson et al., in press). I review the definition of this syndrome as a new Axis-I disorder, named Traumatic Grief. Traumatic Grief occurs after the death of a significant other, which becomes a traumatic separation for the bereaved person. In chapter 3, I explain the criteria for diagnosis in detail and discuss the differential diagnosis. Traumatic Grief conforms to all the characteristics of a mental disorder in DSM-IV. It evolves cohesively over time, and is associated with prolonged disability. Either personal vulnerability, reflected, for example, in a maladaptive attachment style, or socioenvironmental factors such as the violent, horrific circumstances of a death can increase the risk for the disorder. Chapter 4 reviews several other mental disorders that occur at a higher frequency during bereavement and can be comorbid with Traumatic Grief. It is important to recognize and address comorbidity through thorough evaluation and comprehensive, individualized treatment plans.

Traumatic Grief is distinct from other disorders by virtue of unique diagnostic features rooted in the separation anxiety evoked by the death of a significant other, amalgamated with the traumatic devastation caused by the death. Still, Traumatic Grief falls into a broader category of anxiety disorders and has a generic relationship both to Post-traumatic Stress Disorder and Acute Stress Disorder. This is true in the sense that they all occur after an event or experience in a person's life. The landmark experience identified with each of the disorders opens a period of risk for the disorder.

The development of treatments for Traumatic Grief is in a nascent stage. New results from both drug and psychotherapy trials will emerge over the next few years. Still, a review of existing data in chapter 5 indicates the availability of specific or potentially specific psychopharmacologic and psychotherapeutic treatments that enhance the clinician's capacity to help persons afflicted with Traumatic Grief. Given the low risks of treatment and the high potential to help those persons afflicted with Traumatic Grief, in chapter 6, I recommend judicious treatment of the disorder through individualized treatment plans. Also, given the easy identification of the socioenvironmental event causing Traumatic Grief and the known period of risk, I believe there are opportunities for prevention that ought to be incorporated into clinical practice. Accordingly, I discuss the epidemiology of Traumatic Grief and ideas about prevention in chapter 7.

☐ Natural Processes, Healing, and the Helping Professional

As a general proposition, it is important for clinicians to understand and support the natural process of grief, the individual's efforts to cope with the loss, and the social processes of mourning, while fulfilling the role and responsibilities of a professional healer.

One challenge of the diagnosis and treatment of Traumatic Grief is to differentiate normal bereavement from psychopathologic manifestations and processes. Knowledge of normal grief is indispensable to this task. Indeed, corresponding to an axiom for most other disorders and diseases (Bernard, 1957), a true understanding of Traumatic Grief and its treatment rests on a knowledge base of the normal physiology and normal behavior of grief. For this reason, in chapter 1, I have placed the discussion of Traumatic Grief in the context of our growing knowledge of attachment and normal grief.

As I suggested in an earlier text (Jacobs, 1993) that considers Traumatic Grief from the perspective of a disease of adaptation (Dubos, 1965), a complete picture of grief includes the efforts of the bereaved person to cope with a loss (Jacobs, Kasl, Schaefer, & Ostfeld, 1994). The individual's efforts to cope with a death are part of the natural, behavioral process of healing and recovery. In discussing psychotherapy in chapter 6, I indicate how some coping is adaptive and some not. To be as effective as possible, the helping professional must learn to recognize an individual's characteristic coping behaviors and support the roles of the constructive ones in a comprehensive treatment plan, while helping the individual understand how others may be self-defeating. Effective, mutual support groups and other social supports can also nurture and encourage an individual's coping efforts in addition to helping in the search for meaning and providing sentient others with whom to share personal experiences.

An individual's grief evolves in a society that prescribes roles and rituals for the bereaved person and attributes meaning to the death. These social processes have evolved to help and support the bereaved person while maintaining the fabric of society during this period in a person's life when strong, sometimes destructive feelings may emerge. In some cases, these social prescriptions are not best for the individual. In other cases, individuals may be isolated from their extended families and communities. These circumstances may prompt the bereaved person to seek a professional consultation. Whatever the situation, professional care for the bereaved person with clinical complications ought be based n a knowledge of social and cultural variation in meaning, so as to understand how they may be falling short and to intervene in concert with helpful, healing social processes when possible.

☐ Future Developments

Traumatic Grief is an emerging concept and disorder. By virtue of its novelty, it is rapidly developing and potentially controversial. The justification and need for a new nosologic entity and the validity of a new disorder might be questioned and debated in its early stages, thereby raising skepticism about the conclusions reached in this text. Even if controversy is minimal, the diagnostic criteria for this new disorder will evolve more rapidly than for other disorders. New, specific, targeted treatments will appear intermittently over the next few years, outdating the working hypotheses and conclusions developed in chapter 5.

Perhaps it would have been wiser to wait until all the data were in and all the questions were answered before undertaking the task of writing this book. On the other hand, I believe a critical mass of information and data are now available. As a consequence, it is exactly the purpose of this book to alert clinicians sooner rather than later to the importance of Traumatic Grief in their clinical practice and to provide impetus to the process of discovery through clinical research. Admittedly, the timing of this book places a burden to stay current on clinicians who want to understand Traumatic Grief, but I believe that bereaved persons afflicted with Traumatic Grief deserve this attention and effort.

There are two other potential areas for future development that merit consideration: a dimensional approach to diagnosis and losses other than a death.

□   A Dimensional Approach to Diagnosis

At clinical psychiatry's present stage of development, a categorical approach to diagnosis is the norm. Even as we develop the argument for a new diagnostic category called Traumatic Grief in categorical terms, a longer term perspective compels an acknowledgment that a dimensional model of psychopathology (Strauss, 1973) may more accurately represent the continuum between normal and abnormal aspects of grief. Some symptoms, such as identification symptoms or a shattered world view, appear to be qualitatively different from normal experience and fit a categorical model best. Still, many of the symptoms of Traumatic Grief can be understood in relationship to the multiple dimensions of normal grief (discussed in chapter 1) and exist on a continuum of intensity over time. As I have noted repeatedly, a basic and unavoidable challenge in the differential diagnosis of Traumatic Grief is to make judgments about psychopathology during the evolution of the natural process of grief. Given this task, a dimensional model of diagnosis would support the diagnostic task better than a categorical approach through establishment of a continuum. Also, a dimensional model would facilitate examination of the relationship among different dimensions of bereavement, such as emotional distress, social functioning, and perhaps depressive and anxious dimensions. For these reasons, striving for a dimensional approach to definition of Traumatic Grief seems desirable over the long haul.

□   Other Types of Losses

A knowledge of bereavement and Traumatic Grief may prove to be useful for understanding clinical problems that arise during other life experiences in which the theme of loss is relevant. A divorce, the destruction of a home or community, the theft of a prized possession, a long term hospitalization, and other experiences can include a prominent theme of loss. It is also true that other aspects of these experiences lend them a unique character. However, understanding the elements of loss and consequent grief in each experience could make a contribution to clinical understanding and treatment. Although a decision was made by a recent, consensus conference of experts on the diagnosis of Traumatic Grief to limit the diagnosis of Traumatic Grief to the death of a significant other (see chapter 2), with consensus criteria for Traumatic Grief in hand, it is now possible to systematically study whether the same type of reaction occurs after the other types of losses. If this exploration proves fruitful, the implications of this text will extend beyond the diagnosis of Traumatic Grief after the death of a significant other and provide a broader contribution to our understanding of psychopathology and treatment.

☐ References

Bernard, C. (1957). *An introduction to the study of experimental medicine.* New York: Dover Press.

Bowlby, 1969). *Attachment and loss, vol. 1: Attachment.* New York: Basic Books.

Dubos, R. (1965). *Man adapting.* New Haven, CT: Yale University Press.

Jacobs, S. (1993). *Pathologic grief: Maladaptation to loss.* Washington, DC: American Psychiatric Press.

Jacobs, S., Kasl, S., Schaefer, C., & Ostfeld, A. (1994). Conscious and unconscious coping with loss. *Psychosomatic Medicine, 56,* 557–563.

Parkes, C. M. (1972). *Bereavement: Studies of grief in adult life.* New York: International Universities Press.

Prigerson, H. G., Shear, M. K., Jacobs, S. C., Reynolds, C. F., Maciejewski, P. K., Pilkonis, P., Wortman, C., Williams, J. B. W., Widiger, T. A., Davidson, J., Frank, E., Kupfer, D. J., Zisook, S. (in press). Consensus criteria for Traumatic Grief: A preliminary empirical test. *British Journal of Psychiatry.*

Strauss, J. S. (1973). Diagnostic models and the nature of psychiatric disorders. *Archives of General Psychiatry, 29,* 445–449.

INDEX

Acknowledgment, of death, 30
Adaptive coping, 82
Adler, on pathologic grief, 15
Affiliation
    definition of, 4
    neurobiology of, 4–5
Age variation, 91
Alcohol abuse, as comorbidity, 50
Algorithm, diagnosis reatment, 76–87. *See also* Diagnosis reatment algorithm
Alienation, 6
Anger, 31
Anniversaries, of death, 34
Antidepressants, tricyclic
    in adults, 63–64
    author's experience with, 83
    in children and adolescents, 62
    for PTSD, 66
Anxiety disorders, 48. *See also* Generalized Anxiety Disorder; Separation anxiety
    bereavement-specific diagnosis of, 53–54
Attachment, costs and benefits of, 102
Attachment behavior, 2–3
Attachment behavior and theory, 1–13
    behavior in, 2–3
    definition of, 2
    evolution and, 2–3
    history of, 1–2
    in infants and children, 2–3
    neurobiology of affiliation in, 4–5
    psychopathology in, 10–11
    separation anxiety in, 5–10
        after loss, 5–7
        example of, 7–8
        grief and, 8–10
    stimuli for, 3

Avoidance
    of death, 30
    in PTSD, 38

Behavior, attachment, 2–3
Behavior therapies, 69–71
Benzodiazepines, 63
Bowlby
    on bereavement, 15
    on human social relationships, 102
Brief, integrated, problem focused psychotherapy, 81
Brief dynamic psychotherapy (BDP), 68–69, 70–71, 82

Clinical examples
    of comorbidity, 54–56
    of diagnosis, 40–41
    diagnosis reatment algorithm and, 84–87
    of separation anxiety, 7–8
Clinical narrative, 83–84
Cognitive behavioral therapy (CBT), 69, 81–82
    in children, 67
Comorbidity, 45–57
    with alcohol abuse, 50
    clinical examples of, 54–56
    in diagnosis reatment algorithm, 80–81
    with Generalized Anxiety Disorder, 48
    with Major Depressive Disorder, 46–48
    with Panic Disorder, 48
    with Post-traumatic Stress Disorder, 48–50
    with Schizophrenic Disorder, 51
    special considerations in, 53–54
    suicide risk in, 50–51
    Traumatic Grief pathology and, 52–53

Complicated Grief Disorder, 21
Coping, 39–40, 82
  healthy, 104–105
Cortisol excretion, 36
Course of illness, 36
Crisis intervention, 68
Criteria. *See also* Diagnosis
  comparison of, 20–21
  diagnostic, 27, 28t
    consensus, 17–20
    DSM-IV, 21–22
Criterion A, 27–29, 28t
Criterion B, 28t, 29–31
Criterion C, 28t, 32–33
Criterion D, 28t, 33
Cross cultural studies, 91–92
Cultural issues, 91–93
Cultural sanction, 22

Death, of significant other, 27–29, 28t
Definition(s). *See also* specific terms, e.g.,
  Significant other
  of grief, 3
  of separation anxiety, 5
  of traumatic grief, 24
Depression, 14. *See also* Major Depressive
  Disorder
  duration of, 46–47
Descriptive features, 34–35
Desipramine, 52
  in adults, 63–64
  author's experience with, 83
Detachment, 30
Dexamethasone suppression test (DST),
  36
Diagnosis, 27–42
  anniversaries of death and, 34
  circumstances in, 37–41
  clinical example of, 40–41
  course and prognosis in, 36
  criteria for, 27, 28t
    consensus, 17–20
    of Horowitz, 20–21
    proposed, 27, 28t
  death of significant other in, 27–29
  descriptive features in, 34–35
  differential, 36–37
  dimensional approach to, 106
  duration in, 32–33
  general medical conditions in, 35–36
  laboratory findings in, 36

physical findings in, 35–36
  psychosocial impairment in, 33
  separation anxiety symptoms in, 27–29
  symptom severity in, 31–32
  symptoms of traumatization in, 29–31
  variation in pattern, 33–34
Diagnosis reatment algorithm, 76–87
  case examples and, 84–87
  clinical narrative in, 83–84
  comorbidity in, 80–81
  Inventory of Complicated Grief in,
    78–79
  psychotherapy and psychotropic drugs
    in, 81–83
  risk factor evaluation in, 79–80
  signal symptoms in, 77–78
  steps in, 76–81, 77t
  timing and duration in, 79
Differential diagnosis, 36–37
  Generalized Anxiety Disorder, 38
  Major Depressive Disorder, 37
  normal grief, 39–40
  Panic Disorder, 37
  Post-traumatic Stress Disorder, 38–39
  psychotic illness, 39
Dimensional approach, to diagnosis, 106
Disorder, traumatic grief as, 14–24
  consensus diagnostic criteria for, 17–20
  criteria comparison in, 20–21
  cultural sanction in, 21–22
  definition of, 24
  DSM-IV on, 21–22
  nature of, 22–24
  pathologic grief and, 14–17
Drug therapy, 52
  Dosage, 66–67
DSM-IV, 21–22
Duration
  in definition, 18
  in diagnosis, 32–33
  factors in, 31–32
  of Major Depressive Episode, 53
  of psychopharmacology, 66–67
  in treatment decision, 79
Dynamic psychotherapy, 68–69

Emotional numbing, 30
Emptiness, 30
Epidemiology, 89–95
  age and gender in, 91
  costs in, 94

prevalence and incidence in, 89–90
social and cultural issues in, 91–93
utilization of services in, 93–94
Examples, clinical
of comorbidity, 54–56
of diagnosis, 40–41
diagnosis reatment algorithm and,
84–87
of separation anxiety, 7–8
Expression, facial, 35

Facial expression, 35
Family context, 93
Fear
of losing control, 78
separation anxiety and, 3
Feelings
of devastation, 30
of futility, 30
Fluoxetine, 62–63
Freud, on pathologic grief, 14
Futility, feelings of, 30
Future developments, 105–106

Gender, 91
General medical conditions, 35–36
Generalized Anxiety Disorder, 38
as comorbidity, 48
Grief
definition of, 3
manifestations of, 9–10, 9t
normal, 39–40
separation anxiety and, 8–10 (*See also*
Separation anxiety) *vs.* traumatic
stress, 16
Guided mourning, 70

Healing, 104–105
Health utilization, 93–94
Helping profession, 104–105
Horowitz
diagnostic criteria of, 20–21
on pathologic grief, 15–16
on separation distress, 20
Hypnosis, 70–71

Identification
with deceased, 30
symptoms of, 30–31
Imipramine, 62
Impact of Events Scale, 16

Incidence, 90
Interpersonal psychotherapy (IPT), 69, 81
Inventory of Complicated Grief (ICG), 18
in diagnosis reatment algorithm, 78–79
Traumatic Grief Evaluation of
Response to Loss in, 97
Irritability, 31
Isolation, in attachment behavior, 2

Laboratory findings, 36
Lindeman, on pathologic grief, 15
Loss, separation anxiety after, 5–7

Major Depressive Disorder, 37
as comorbidity, 46–48
Major Depressive Episode
bereavement-specific diagnosis of, 53
as comorbidity
clinical example of, 54–55
in diagnosis reatment algorithm, 80
Meaninglessness, 30
Medical conditions, general, 35–36
Medication, treatment, 66–67
Multimodal treatment, 83
Mutual support groups, 72–73, 82–83

Narrative, clinical, 83–84
Natural processes, 104–105
Neurobiology, of affiliation, 4–5
Nortriptyline, 52
in adults, 63–65
author's experience with, 83
Numbness, 30

Pang of grief, 15
Panic Disorder, 37
as comorbidity, 48, 81
Paroxetine, 52, 64–65
Pathologic grief, 14–17
Physical findings, 35–36
Pining, 6
Post-traumatic Stress Disorder (PTSD),
14–15, 38–39
bereavement-specific diagnosis of,
53–54
as comorbidity, 48–50
clinical example of, 55–56
in diagnosis reatment algorithm, 80
psychopharmacology for, 66
Prevalence, 89–90
Prevention, 95–98
risk factors in, 94–95

Prigerson, on traumatic grief, 16–18
Primum non nocere, 60–61
Profession, helping, 104–105
Prognosis, 36
Psychopharmacology, 62–67
    in adults and elderly, 63–65
    in diagnosis reatment algorithm, 81–83
    medication, dosage, and duration in,
        66–67
    for Post-traumatic Stress Disorder, 66
    for Separation Anxiety Disorder, 62–63
    studies on, 66
Psychosocial impairment, 33, 78
Psychotherapy, 52–53, 67–73
    in adults, 68–71
        behavior therapies, 69–71
        brief dynamic psychotherapy,
            68–69
        crisis intervention, 68
        self-help groups, 72–73
        summary of studies on, 71–72
    brief, integrated, problem focused
        psychotherapy, 81
    in diagnosis reatment algorithm, 81–83
    for Separation Anxiety Disorder, 67–73
Psychotic illness, 39
PTSD. *See* Post-traumatic Stress Disorder
Purposelessness, 30

Raphael, on grief and trauma, 16
Risk factors, 94–95
    evaluation of, 79–80

Schizophrenic Disorder, 51
Searching, 29
Searching behavior, 5–6
Selective serotonin reuptake inhibitors
    (SSRIs)
    in adults, 65
    author's experience with, 83
    in children and adolescents, 62
    for PTSD, 66
Self-help groups, 72–73, 82–83
Separation anxiety
    after loss, 5–7
    definition of, 5
    in diagnosis, 29
    example of, 7–8
    facial expression of, 35
    grief and, 2, 8–10
    in Post-traumatic Stress Disorder, 38
    symptoms of, 27–29

Separation Anxiety Disorder, 23–24
    Traumatic Grief as, 61–62
    treatment of
        psychopharmacology in, 62–63
        psychotherapy in, 67–73
Separation distress, 6–7, 16
    Horowitz on, 20
Separation pain, 6
Severity, of symptoms, 31–32
Shock, 30
Signal symptoms, 77–78
Significant other
    death of, 27–29, 28t
    definition of, 29
Social and cultural issues, 91–93
Stress. *See* Post-traumatic Stress Disorder
Suicidal ideation, 78
Suicide, risk of, 50–51
Symptoms
    of deceased, assumption of, 30–31
    multiple, 34–35
    severity of, 31–32
    signal, 77–78
    of traumatization by death, 29–31
    variations in patterns, 33–39

Timing, in treatment decision, 79
Trauma desensitization, 70–71
Traumatic Grief Evaluation of Response to
    Loss (TRGER2L), 97
Traumatic stress, *vs.* grief, 16
Treatment, 60–73
    conservatism in, 60–61
    multimodal, 83
    overview of, 61–62
    philosophy of, 60–61
    psychopharmacology in, 62–67 (*See
        also* Psychopharmacology)
    psychotherapy in, 67–73 (*See also*
        Psychotherapy)
    specific interventions in, 52
Treatment algorithm, 76–87. *See also*
    Diagnosis reatment algorithm
Tricyclic antidepressants
    in adults, 63–64
    author's experience with, 83
    in children and adolescents, 62
    for PTSD, 66
Tucker, on clinical narrative, 83–84

Utilization of services, 93–94

World view, shattered, 30